# Student Handbook for Business Management and Administration

**Geoffrey Whitehead, BSc (Econ)**
**Graham Whitehall, BA (Hons) (Econ)**

The Institute of Commercial Management

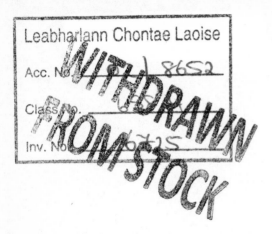
First published in 1989 by Hutchinson Education
New edition 2000
Reprinted 2000

Published by
The Institute of Commercial Management
PO Box 125, Christchurch, Dorset BH23 IYP, England
Tel: +44(0)1202 490555  Fax: +44(0)1202 490666
Email: instcm@instcm.co.uk  Website: http://www.instcm.co.uk

**British Library Cataloguing in Publication Data**
A catalogue record for this book is available from the British Library

ISBN 1 903260 01 9
Printed and bound in Great Britain at The Bath Press, Bath

# Preface

This *Student Handbook for Business Management and Administration* is to be used in conjunction with the core textbook, *Business Management and Administration*. The study scheme of the *Handbook* is introduced in Chapter 1, where the various activities are described.

At the start of the *Handbook,* we have included some general study and examination tips. More mature readers may feel that such advice is not very helpful to them. Please feel free to move on to the body of the text if you wish to do so.

The *Handbook* includes a wealth of material designed to reinforce your study of the main text and to give you adequate practice in expressing yourself about the subject of Business Management and Administration. We wish all students every success on this demanding course.

Geoffrey Whitehead
Graham Whitehall

# Contents

# General study and exam tips

Being successful on a course does not simply result from listening to lectures or reading a textbook. You must become actively involved in the learning process in order to acquire knowledge and skills and perform well in assessments.

There is no reason why you cannot achieve this aim. After all, you are on a course of study because an examining authority believes that you have the necessary ability to complete the course successfully. If you are prepared to become actively involved and do the work required, you have every right to feel confident that you can succeed in the final examinations.

These notes are designed to make your study more efficient, to ensure that you use this manual to best advantage and to help you improve both your coursework and your examination techniques. They have been divided into four parts:

1  general study tips
2  improving the quality of your work
3  examination technique
4  studying with this text.

## 1  General study tips

An eminent physicist once said: 'Thinking is 99 percent perspiration and 1 percent inspiration.' Take his advice and ignore fellow students who believe you can prepare yourself for the examination in one or two weeks before the final examinations. Knowledge and skills of any value are not easily learned. For most of us it takes time to understand and digest the content of a subject. Therefore start to study seriously right at the very start of your course and continue at a steady pace until the examinations. Do all the work expected of you by your tutor including homework and mock/mid-term examinations. Homework is good practice and the mock exams simulate aspects of the final examination. Doing them as well as possible makes your tutor more willing to help you, as he or she will see that you are playing your part in the learning process.

The knowledge and skills you will gain on your course of study are precisely the kind needed by professional business people. Approach the study of each subject as if you were in real life a business man or woman, or a person following a profession such as accountancy or law. In this way the subject should come alive for you, and your motivation to learn should increase.

To help realise this objective, read a quality daily and Sunday newspaper that has a good business section. By doing this you will discover what is happening in the wider world on a day-to-day basis and be in a better position to understand the topics you are studying on the course. You will also broaden and deepen your knowledge of the subjects you are studying. Professional people at work usually read a quality newspaper and a monthly or quarterly periodical related directly to their discipline in order to keep abreast of the latest developments. You will probably wish to do the same when you commence work, so why not start now? *The Economist* is one of the best journals in this respect. It gives worldwide coverage of all aspects of business. Carry a pocket dictionary with you and look up words you hear or read but do not understand. None of us has a complete vocabulary but we can improve it if we really want to be able to read and study more effectively.

As soon as you start any course, make sure you have been given a syllabus of each subject you are to study. The syllabus for Business Management and Administration appears at the end of this section of general study advice. The syllabus is a detailed list of the topics you are to study during your course. They will usually be grouped together under sub-headings, and these sub-headings make an excellent framework for your studies. Buy a lever arch file (not a ring binder) and a couple of packets of page dividers. Both these items are very cheap and available at most stationers. You also need a cheap two-hole punch. Use the page dividers to separate your work in each of the sub-headings. As your course proceeds each section should build into a complete study of that sub-section of your syllabus. It will contain any notes you have made, any essays you have had marked, any answers you wrote to questions (whether they were marked or not). It will also contain any important articles you have cut out from journals relevant to the subject, and so on. Make a point of keeping any wise sayings you read or hear at lectures, especially any funny ones. A joke can often lighten an otherwise dull subject.

Eventually you will need a lever arch file for each subject, but for day-to-day use keep a file which has room for all your subjects. As you move on from one main topic to the next, clear the material for a completed sub-heading into the main file for that subject. Throw away any odd notes or other rubbish and you have a clean collection of material for revision at a later date.

If you do not understand something ask your tutor. Do not assume that you are inadequate because you did not understand something that other students seemed to appreciate. They may be having difficulties too, or your lecturer may simply not have explained the point to everyone's satisfaction. If something is overlooked by the tutor, do not be afraid to bring it to his/her attention.

Personal health is something that many students dismiss with comments such as: 'What has health got to do with the ability to think?' Studies on the topic have now clearly indicated that general health and mental performance are statistically related. Within four weeks of being given multi-vitamin and mineral tablets, students in two separate controlled studies improved upon their written performance in intelligence tests by approximately 10 points. Your common sense alone should tell you that you cannot perform at your best if you continually feel tired or have 'flu or a heavy cold in an examination. Eat a varied diet that includes protein foods, vegetables and fruit, and get some daily exercise even if it is only a good brisk walk home after your day's study. Contrary to the belief of many students, the best academic work is not done at night-time. Once again research shows that students perform better in the early part of the week, in the daytime – particularly mornings – and in a place where there is natural daylight to read and write by. Plan your study schedule so that it is completed in the day. This will also leave you the evenings and weekends free to relax and enjoy yourself.

# 2 Improving the quality of your work

The earlier in the course you bring your work to a satisfactory standard the more likely you are to exhibit a good standard of work in final examinations. Obviously, academic standards relate to the thinking abilities of the student but they also depend on motivation, and a logical approach to one's work, if effective presentation at the appropriate academic standard is to be achieved. Here are three tips that will help you develop a logical approach to the presentation of your work.

## Read the question carefully

When undertaking an essay or numerical work make sure you read the question very carefully. Underline the key words in the question so that your mind is concentrated on the essential aspects. For example, distinguish between the two main types of question.

### Descriptive questions
A descriptive question is one in which you will be expected to describe or explain something and possibly distinguish it from alternative or similar items or ideas. Two examples are:
1 *Describe and distinguish above-the-line advertising* from other forms of *advertising*.
2 *Explain* with the *aid of graphs, how the price* of a product is *determined* in a highly *competitive economy*.
    Some of the key words have been emphasised in italics to give you an idea of which words are at the heart of the question. Always underline or highlight the key words yourself before attempting to answer.

### Analytical questions
These include the purely analytical question, or the analytical question that requires you to evaluate a statement (indicate your level of support for an idea/give it a value) or only to present your own ideas. Examples of these are:
1 *Solely analytical* Analyse the contention that there is no such thing as fixed costs.
2 *Analytical and evaluative* How far do you support the idea that the adult behaviour is predominantly related to one's early childhood experience?
    If you have been presented with a mini-case (scenario) or case study (extended story) detailing opposing opinions regarding a problem a company is faced with, you may be requested to offer your own solution. In this event your answer should analyse the value of all the opinions offered in the case as well as suggesting your own.

Consider also the way a question is structured. If it is in two or more parts, give equal time to each if equal marks are awarded to each part. If more marks are awarded to one part than another, allocate your time in the same proportion as the marks. For example, if a question awards 5 marks for part (a) and 15 marks for part (b) (total 20 marks), you should spend a quarter (5/20) of your time answering (a) and three-quarters (15/20) on (b).

Sometimes the time you should allocate to a part of a question is indicated by the implied requirements of the question, rather than by marks. For example:

Q1 a Briefly outline 'actual' and 'ostensible' authority.

   b Brown and Brown Ltd contracted with a married woman for the laying of new carpets. After the work had been done the woman's husband refuted the contract and refused to pay for the carpets. Advise Brown and Brown Ltd and the woman on their legal positions.

By using the words 'briefly outline' the examiner is indicating that much less time should be spent on answering part (a). The question requires more marks to be awarded to part (b) as the analytical and applied nature of this part indicates that it is more difficult to answer. A good rule is to ask yourself whether you have exhausted the possibilities of the question. If you are asked to give reasons why, and so on, and you give two reasons when in fact there could be eight good possible reasons, you will only get two-eighths of the marks (a clear failure). An American visitor passed two Cambridge dons in earnest discussion as they walked round the quadrangle. All he heard were the words 'and ninthly…' Clearly the gentleman was exhausting the possibilities of the matter under discussion!

With numerical questions, such as in accountancy and statistics, do not assume that all you have to do is arrive at the right answer. Your tutor – or an examiner – will expect you to explain what you are doing as you introduce each set of workings, graphs, illustrations or tables. After all, how is your tutor to know how you arrived at the right answer if you do not explain? Even more importantly, even if you give the wrong answer, at least you will be given some marks for those parts of your calculation which are correct. Such subjects involve a large element of communication and, if you do not communicate effectively in your answer what you are doing, you will lose marks.

## Construct an essay plan

Always spend a few minutes constructing an essay plan before answering a question. This only requires jotting down a few notes for each paragraph which indicates the approach you will take to your answer and the points you will include. This will make sure that you construct your essay in a logical manner and that you keep to a target when writing your answer.

## Follow up with your tutor

To understand fully what is required when answering questions, ask your tutor about the work you have handed in and had marked if he or she has not commented sufficiently on your script, informing you of where you were right and wrong and why.

# 3   Examination technique

If you are studying at college you can start improving your examination technique in the mock/mid-term examination which will help you in the coursework assessment during the second half of the course as well as in the final examination. Here are a few tips on improving your presentation.

- *Always do rough workings.* Use essay plans and/or numerical workings to plan your answer, but on a page other than the one on which you start your answer to the question. Cross through your rough working before starting to answer the question.
- Select the questions you intend to answer and *start with the one you think you will find the easiest to answer.* In this way you may gain your higher marks early in the exam, which is very important in case you do not complete the examination.
- *Keep an eye on the clock* so that you allow about the same amount of time for answering each question (unless one is a more difficult, compulsory question). Noting the time in order to complete all the questions you are required to answer gives you a better chance of achieving high marks.
- Allow at least one third to half a page for illustrations or diagrams. In this way they look like illustrations rather than scribblings and you have sufficient space available if you have to return to your illustration to add more detail later in the examination. Always explain what you illustration is supposed to illustrate.
- Unless otherwise instructed, use a complete page of graph paper for presenting graphs and make sure that you provide a title for any entries you have made. Explain what your graph illustrates.
- Do not present workings for numerical subjects such as accounts and statistics without explaining what you are doing and why.

# 4   Studying with the main text

The main text has been specifically designed to act as a study aid to students while on a course, as well as to present the contents of a subject in a way that is both interesting and informative.

Use this text as part of your study activities, adding your own or your tutor's notes at appropriate points. Study your textbook in great detail, making notes on the chief points in each chapter so that the ideas have gone through your own head and down onto the paper in your own words, though perhaps with key quotations from the text.

Do not get bogged down in any one chapter. If you really cannot follow the chapter, leave it and go on to the next, returning at a later date. What seems difficult at the start of your course in September will be easier by December and child's play by March! You are going to develop as you do the course, so do not give up too early. Perseverance is everything in acquiring professional status.

At the end of each chapter of the main text you should turn to the Students Handbook. Chapter 1 of the handbook explains the approaches we have adopted.

Briefly these may be listed as follows:

a  A set of revision questions in Question and Answer form, to consolidate your knowledge of the chapter.

b  A set of self-assessment questions to recall the subject matter and give you a chance to express yourself about various aspects.

c  A project or assignment which you may like to try. Such activities take you out of a 'textbook study' atmosphere and give you a chance to explore real life situations.

d  Sets of examination questions requiring answers in greater depths than the self-assessment questions mentioned above.

Now that you have read these study and exam tips you should feel confident to continue with your studies and succeed in the examinations. It just remains for us to wish you every success on your course.

## Your syllabus – business management & administration

*Part A – the organisational background to business administration*

### The Management Framework to Business Administration

What is Business Administration? • What is Management? • The Board of Directors • Functions within an Organisation • The 'Systems' Approach to Organisation • Planning-Control Feedback Cycles

### Characteristic features of organisations

The Structure of Organisations • The Need for Authority • The Features of Bureaucratic Organisation • Non-Bureaucratic Organisations • The Principles of Organisation • Types of Organisation • More about Systems & Subsystems

### The structure of business enterprises

The Pattern of Organisations • Sole-Trader Enterprises • Partnerships • Limited Partnerships • The Limited Liability Company • Non-Profit-Making Units (Clubs & Societies) • Public Enterprises • Autonomous Public Corporations • Nationalised Industries • Local Government Institutions • Central Government Departments

*Part B – functions within organisations*

### The production function

The Production Process • Types of Production • Site Selection & Factory Planning • Plant & Equipment • Materials & Materials Handling • Production Administration • Costing Aspects of Production • Work Study • Maintenance & Production

### The purchasing function

The Nature of Purchasing • The Role of the Purchasing Officer • Purchasing Department Procedures • Inventory Control • Stores Control • Economic Order Quantity

### The research & development function

The Functions of the Research & Development Department • Basic Research • Problem-Based Research • Ideas Generation • Applied Research & Development • Patents, Trade Marks & Service Marks • Research & Development in the Business Organisation

### The marketing function

Introduction to Marketing • The Marketing Philosophy • Market Analysis & Research • Promotion, Publicity & Public Relations • Pricing Policy • Credit Control • Sales Administration • Transport & Distribution

### The information technology function

Introduction to Information Technology • The Telephone System • The Characteristics of Computers • The Computer as a Local Area Network – LAN • LANS, VANS and WANS • The Need for Worldwide Links • The Intranet, the Extranet and the Internet • Secure 'E'Commerce • Role of the Admin Officer

### Personnel department

The Need for Staff • The Functions of the Personnel Department • A Personnel Policy • Employee Records • Promotion & Transfer • Termination & Dismissal • Industrial Relations Practice • The Remuneration of Staff

## Part C – the administrative officer's role

### Office administration

The Role of the Administrative Officer • Facilities Management – The 'New-Look' Office Administrator • The Office & its Functions • The Clerical Function • Business Correspondence • Mail Inwards • Mail Outwards • Systems for Producing Business Correspondence • Meetings • Conferences & Functions • Delegation

### Other responsibilities of the administration

The Organisation and Methods Department • Security Aspects of Business • Risk Management • The Environment of Business • The Concept of Claimants

## Reading list

### Main text

Organisation & Administration for Business –
G Whitehead and G. Whitehall (Institute of Commercial Management)

### Alternative texts and further reading

Modern Business Administration – RC Appleby (Pitman) ISBN 0273 602 829
The Structure of Business – M Buckley (Pitman) ISBN 0273 602 691

# 1 The management framework to business administration

## 1.1 Revision tests

In this student handbook each chapter begins with a revision test which reminds you of the subject matter discussed in the same chapter of the main text. If you have not read Chapter One of the main text read it now before you start this revision test.

The test is in an unusual format, which we call a 'teach and test' format. If you take a sheet of paper or a piece of thin card and lay it across the page to cover up everything but the first question you will find it asks 'What is business administration?' You can try to answer this, but if you get stuck slide the paper down and read the answer. Then go on to Question 2. The idea is that the first few times you are teaching yourself the answers to the questions. Later on, just before your examinations you can use the test to revise your subject, and the answers will come back into your head because you have been at great pains to learn the material earlier on your course.

## 1.2 Revision test: business administration

| Answers | Questions |
|---|---|
| | 1 What is business administration? |
| 1 It is that part of a business organisation which seeks to implement the decisions made by the top management and achieve the objectives it has specified. | 2 What is management? |
| 2 It is the process of determining the objectives of a company and laying down policies and systems of organisation which will achieve the objectives specified. | 3 Which body exercises overall control of a limited company? |
| 3 The board of directors. | 4 Name some members of the board of directors, and their functions. |

| Answers | Questions |
|---|---|
| 4 (a) Chairman – in charge of all board meetings;<br>(b) managing director – a full-time executive running the day-to-day affairs of the company<br>(c) executive directors – members of the board who are also full-time executives and usually heads of departments like marketing, production, personnel, and so on<br>(d) part-time (non-executive) directors – who have expert knowledge or experience in particular fields. | **5 What are the functions of the board of directors?** |
| 5 (a) To formulate policy on all matters affecting the company<br>(b) to make plans so that the objectives of the company are realised<br>(c) to set up an appropriate organisation and appoint suitably qualified staff<br>(d) to comply with the Companies Acts and all other statutory requirements<br>(e) to ensure the financial stability of the company by a regular review of its financial affairs<br>(f) many more – but the chief function of the board is to give leadership. | **6 What are the chief types of authority?** |
| 6 (a) *De jure* or line authority conferred by senior management as part of the process of delegation<br>(b) *de facto* authority, conceded by equals and subordinates in recognition of the manager's personal qualities. | **7 What is a planning-control feedback cycle?** |
| 7 A system of work which permits the detailed planning of every aspect of a firm's activity, and subjects every process to control procedures which test it out, and establish the quality and standard of performance achieved, thus enabling progress reports to be made to management so that corrections can be applied if necessary. | **8 What is a 'systems' approach to the management of organisations?** |
| 8 One which regards the organisation as a system for achieving certain desirable objectives within an environment of economic or social needs. | **9 What is the importance of the systems approach?** |
| 9 It enables the manager to move out of the narrow tunnel of line management, and see the needs of the whole system more clearly. He/she will consider the chain of effects following from his/her decisions as they interact on other subsystems in the organisation. | **10 What is meant by the life-cycle concept?** |
| 10 It is a concept that holds that all products and services have only a limited life, and must eventually be replaced by alternative products or services, perhaps reflecting the use of new materials, new forms of communication etc. | **11 Go over the list again, until you are sure of the answers. Then try the self-assessment questions in Section 1.3 below.** |

# 1.3 Self-assessment questions in this handbook

On any educational course tutors set a number of pieces of class work and homework for students. Often called 'assignments', these pieces of work are clearly very important and much of your grading by the lecturer concerned depends on the quality of the assignments you submit. To avoid overloading the lecturer with marking the number of assignments is kept down and it often happens that the best students need to do far more than the set programme. 'Writing maketh an exact man' said Francis Bacon (1561–1626). Only if you do plenty of writing will you develop your style, and your vocabulary, and succeed in using the exact words you need to make your point correctly in any essay, thesis or report.

All this extra work cannot be marked by your tutor, but it can be assessed by you. The process of self-assessment is simple. Having set down your views on any matter ask yourself.
- How good an answer have I written?
- Have I set down my ideas simply and clearly?
- Have I exhausted the possibilities of the question, or are there some aspects I have overlooked?
- Is the spelling correct, and is the punctuation sound, and so on and so on.

Then give yourself a mark for it out of 100. Write the mark on your paper, preceded by the letters SA (for Self Assessment).

In each chapter of this book you will find a set of self-assessment questions. You should answer these as fully as you can. The answers supplied lower down (in section 1.7 for example) are necessarily only abbreviated.

Later in the chapter you will find some specimen answers. They aren't necessarily very full answers – space does not permit – but your own answers should be as full as your time allows.

# 1.4 Self-assessment questions

(Answers at 1.7 below)

Here are nine questions about Chapter 1 in the main text. Take a sheet of paper and do what is required in each case. Then go through the self-assessment procedure for each question and give yourself a mark out of 100. File these sheets for revision later.
1 Define business administration.
2 What is the link between the board of a company and the body of employees who carry out company activities?
3 What is management?
4 What is the composition of a board of directors?
5 What are the functions of a board of directors?
6 What are the main functions of an organisation?
7 What is meant by 'a systems approach to organisation'?

8  'A manager should see problems embedded in every decision he makes.' Explain what this means.
9  What is a life-cycle? Refer in your answer to products used in your everyday life.

## 1.5    Projects in this Student Workbook

A project is an in-depth study of a particular area of a syllabus, in which the student is set free to pursue the subject in any way he/she likes. An imaginative student will produce a really interesting portfolio of material. Other students find projects tedious and difficult. as a matter of fact projects are more appropriate to other areas of study than Business Administration – say History or Geography. They are inserted here in each chapter, but we recommend that you only pick one or two in your college year. Read through the rest but do not overburden yourself with project work.

## 1.6    An assignment on the life-cycle of a product

The ten-year life-cycle of a particular product has been divided by the planning department into the following phases:
Phase 1:  Specification and outline approval
2:  Design and tooling up
3:  Production and marketing
4:  First revamping
5:  Second revamping
6:  Phasing out
Suggest at least five problems for each phase which might need to be considered and solved.

## 1.7    Answers to self-assessment questions

1  Business administration is that part of the management of a business organisation which seeks to implement the decisions of top management and achieve the objectives which top management has specified.
2  The link is the managing director, who implements the board's policies in practice through the staff, and reports back to the board on progress and problems.
3  The answer to this question is given in *italic* type in section 1.2, p. 4 of the textbook.
4  The board consists of a chairman, a deputy chairman, the managing director, a number of executive directors and a number of part-time directors.

5  The board has many functions but the chief ones are:
   a to decide the objectives of the company and formulate plans to achieve them
   b to establish a proper organisation and appoint suitable senior staff
   c to ensure compliance with the law, particularly the Companies Acts, the Health and
     Safety at Work Act, and so on
   d to provide and supervise the finances of the company, its capital adequacy, cash flows
     and audit of the finances
   e to ensure a high level of morale among staff at all times.
6  The main functions of an organisation are to pursue the objectives for which it was set
   up. These vary with the organisation, but for most manufacturing and commercial
   enterprises they would involve manufacturing and trading in a particular field with a
   view to earning profits as a result of the enterprise shown. For non-profit-making enterprises, and for such institutions as government departments, local authority organisations, and so on, the motivation would not be to achieve profits but to provide the
   services required in their particular fields.
      Within these general aims there will be set up a range of functional departments to
   carry out the various activities needed. For example, production department, purchasing department and marketing department will fulfil these essential functions for most
   trading enterprises. Most organisations will need a personnel department and an
   accounts department, while routine activities such as reception, clerical and secretarial
   services, motor vehicles, meetings, conferences and so on would be arranged through
   the general administration department.
7  A systems approach to organisation means that we regard any organisation as being
   made up of a number of systems of work which will together realise the objectives laid
   down by top management. Thus we have a system for designing the products, and for
   testing them, and for dealing with complaints, and for answering the correspondence.
   A bottleneck in one system will have an adverse effect on the other systems and managers must be alert to see troubles ahead and take steps to avoid them before they have
   a chance to occur.
8  When a manager makes a decision he/she must only make it if the full effects have been
   envisaged. All the possible consequences that will follow must be considered. Thus a
   rise for shopfloor workers may lead to other demands from other staff and cost far more
   than the manager envisaged when the increase was conceded.
9  Every product goes through a life-cycle. First it is new, and in demand. Sales will build
   to a peak but may eventually fall away. At this point we may revive it by a new image –
   for example, repackaging. Eventually sales will tail off and the item will be discontin-
   ued. Good examples are pop records, fashion items for ladies, children's toys, popular
   novels, and so on.

## 1.8   Examination questions in this book

To answer questions well in the final examinations is the key to success. You cannot do it well if:

i   You haven't mastered the subject matter of your course by steady application from the very start. Do not cut lectures; attend every session and help to make it a lively one.

ii   Your vocabulary, spelling, mastery of the language if it is not your own, style of writing, etc are defective. You cannot master all these things in the last month of your course. Start right away; get to know how to use a thesaurus (treasury of words), dictionary, the index of your main text, etc. etc.

iii You haven't written plenty of answers to specimen examination questions. Practice makes perfect. If you start writing answers to examination questions at Chapter One, by the end of your course you will be writing really good answers.

In this book there is a section of examination questions at the end of each chapter. Answer one or two of them before you go on to the next chapter, but also return to them in your revision periods before monthly tests, end-of-session tests etc to do one or two more. Writing examination answers is one of the best ways of revising. It concentrates the mind; helps you to recall what a particular chapter was all about and over the months helps you produce essays which are of the right quality professionally.

## 1.9   Examination questions

1   Draw an organisation chart showing at least five important line functions and four levels of authority within an organisation.

2   What is meant by each of the terms below when used in connection with organisation? Write about 8–10 lines on each.
    a Functions
    b Authority
    c Executive directors
    d Feedback cycles

3   What functions are performed by a board of directors? Refer in your answer to either a limited company organisation or a public sector corporation.

4   Explain the value of the 'systems approach' to organisations, outlining how a manager's attitude might be improved by adopting this approach in his/her work.

5   'It is the function of a board of directors to set objectives for a company, or a group of companies, both in the long term and the immediate short term. It is the task of the managing director to achieve the objectives set.' Discuss the purpose of setting objectives, and their value in an established company.
    (Note: The framework of an answer to this question is given below.)

6   'The work of the chief executive is of central importance to the effectiveness of any organisation.' What role does the chief executive undertake?

# 1.10 Study tips: guide to the answer to question 5

1  In answering this question we need a discussion of the board's duties to set objectives. Students should explain that if a company has long-term and medium-term objectives which the board has discussed and decided upon as attainable targets, it gives everyone a yardstick from which to measure the activities of the company and to motivate both themselves and those below them. Even a well-established company needs to set targets for future growth, consolidation of areas already developed and preparation for new targets for the future. The managing director is the link between the board and the ordinary employees, and has to convey the objectives to lower personnel and see that the targets set by the board are devolved into departmental and personal objectives.

2  a The purpose of setting objectives is staff motivation. The board sets out the broad aims for the whole company.

   b The implications of these aims for departments are then discussed and a plan for achieving them is drawn up. Staff become involved in agreeing departmental objectives.

   c These then devolve into personal standards to be achieved – the level of performance being essentially attainable but requiring effort.

   d The achievement of the objective is an influence on salary, promotion and career prospects.

3  The effect on management can be helpful – they have to set standards, to define objectives in terms meaningful to their staff, to collect feedback material and initiate corrective action. Staff may need to remonstrate with the managing director and feed back to the board the impossibility of the targets set – or their impossibility as dynamic events alter the possibilities.

4  The effect on shopfloor staff is also important – some will cooperate, others will be resentful. Some monetary incentive or at least career development incentive may be necessary.

# 2 Characteristic features of organisations

## 2.1 Revision test: features of business organisation

(To consolidate your knowledge of Chapter 2 in the main text)

| Answers | Questions |
|---|---|
| | 1 What are the three types of authority? |
| 1 (a) Charismatic authority<br>(b) traditional authority<br>(c) legal authority. | 2 Which types of organisation display charismatic authority? |
| 2 Organisations led by their original founders or by outstanding personalities who have pursued an individual line against the conventions of an established system. | 3 Which types of organisation display traditional authority? |
| 3 Established small-scale systems, for example family firms run on patriarchal lines. | 4 What is meant by 'legal' authority? |
| 4 Authority laid down by an agreed procedure, which may in fact be fully legal, drawing its authority from Parliament or some other legislature, but in most cases is purely procedural, brought about by passing resolutions in committees, and so on, and thus establishing a code of rules approved in some formal manner. | 5 What do we call the type of organisation based on legal authority? |
| 5 Bureaucratic. | 6 What are the chief features of bureaucratic organisation? |
| 6 (a) It is impersonal, not personal.<br>(b) Individuals are appointed to 'offices' and their authority come from being an 'official'.<br>(c) Obedience is to the office and not to the individual.<br>(d) Each office has its sphere of competence, within which it is empowered to act according to rules laid down previously.<br>(e) The structure of the organisation is hierarchical. Information flows up the hierarchy and instructions flow down again. | 7 What is the most fully-developed form of bureaucratic organisation? |

| Answers | Questions |
|---|---|
| (f) Obedience to superiors and behaviour within the guidelines are a condition of membership of the organisation. | |
| 7 The multidivisional company. | **8 What are its features?** |
| 8 (a) Each division operates as a separate company in its own field, where it seeks to play a dominant role. <br> (b) The aim is to increase market share and make super-profits as a result of the economies of large scale. <br> (c) At corporate level a team of top executives monitor the work of the divisions and assess the effectiveness of the chief executive of each division. <br> (d) Below the chief executive, layers of middle management feed instructions down the line and grass-roots opinions and changing circumstances up the line. | **9 What proved to be the defects of the multidivisional company in the 'nanosecond nineties'?** |
| 9 (a) Fierce competition from the NICs (newly industrialised countries) began to erode the markets of the multidivisional companies. <br> (b) In particular, they lost the entrepreneurial spirit (choked off by the burdensome on-costs of bloated management overheads). | **10 What is an organismic structure?** |
| 10 It is one where employees are expected to display a lively interest in the success of the entire enterprise, not just their own specialist department. | **11 What are the features of an organismic structure?** |
| 11 (a) They are based on commitment to the total task facing the organisation. <br> (b) A wide communication pattern of information and advice is established so that all know the 'real world' of the organisation. <br> (c) The structure of the organisation is a network, with knowledge on particular matters lying at many points in the network and accessible to all. <br> (d) Individuals are motivated by the desire to advance the total level of achievement of the organisation and achieve client satisfaction. | **12 What is the 'human relations' movement?** |
| 12 A movement which seeks to arrange production in such a way that the individual is able to realise his/her psychological needs (self-esteem, the esteem of others and self-realisation) as well as his/her economic needs. | **13 What sort of company is now appearing out of the remains of the multidivisional company?** |
| 13 The entrepreneurial company. | **14 What are its features?** |
| 14 (a) The emphasis is on enterprise: to develop new products and new services which will be competitive on a world-wide scale. <br> (b) Emphasis is placed also upon the value of every member of staff – all skills are needed. Everyone is empowered to take decisions and act in the interests of the company and for the good of the company as a whole. | **15 What are the principles of organisation?** |

| Answers | Questions |
|---|---|
| (c) The leading personalities issue a mission statement and a strategy to be followed, which rolls forward as the years pass. <br> (d) Elimination of many layers of middle management reduces frustration of grass-roots staff and cuts overheads to improve the competitive state of the business. <br> (e) The organisation is a flatter, de-layered one, with better communication between all staff, more training to ensure all know the aims and objectives of the company, and thus can make decisions along the right lines, without constant reference to supervisory grades (which no longer exist). | |
| 15 (a) Define the objectives. <br> (b) Decide what work is involved and group it into areas of responsibility. <br> (c) Designate posts and define their responsibilities. <br> (d) Accord each post a level of authority appropriate to it. <br> (e) Draw up and publish statements of policy and codes of conduct. | **16 What are the main types of organisation?** |
| 16 (a) Line organisations. <br> (b) Line and staff organisations. <br> (c) Functional organisations. <br> (d) Organismic organisations. | **17 What is a 'loop'?** |
| 17 It is a control procedure which compares actual results with original objectives and loops back to adjust the system where it is failing to achieve the original aim in quality, quantity, cost or some other objective. | **18 Go over the page again until you are sure of the points made. Then try the self-assessment questions below.** |

# 2.2   Self-assessment questions

(Answers on p. 11)

Here are 12 questions about Chapter 2 in the main text. Take a sheet of paper and do what is required in each case. Then go through the self-assessment procedure for each question and give yourself a mark out of 100. File these sheets for revision later.

1   What is client dissatisfaction? Why is it likely to be easily reduced in a town centre shopping area, and less easily reduced in a welfare office?
2   Explain charismatic authority.
3   Explain traditional authority.
4   Explain legal authority.
5   You have been appointed to a minor post of special responsibility in a manufacturing firm, with a particular interest in processing export cargoes. Explain your position in the organisation, with particular reference to your authority.

6 Who will define the objectives of an organisation?
7 How will these objectives be promulgated?
8 A post is advertised in general terms and letters arrive expressing interest. What should we send to the applicants so that they can make formal application?
9 Distinguish between line organisation and functional organisation.
10 What are the basic features of a multidivisional company?
11 What are the basic features of an entrepreneurial company?
12 What are loop controls?

## 2.3 A project on business organisation

Make a detailed study of your own workplace, whatever it is, and pinpoint how it is organised. Use the names of official positions(for example, manager, supervisor, chief clerk, and so on) rather than the names of individuals. Indicate any chains of command which appear to exist. For those in full-time education, study the department in which you are following your main course. Assess the effectiveness of the organisation you have studied and bring out clearly its strengths and its weaknesses. Keep the discussion of such matters impersonal, and consider them objectively (from the point of view of an outsider who is not personally involved). Present your analysis and report as a small portfolio of work done.

## 2.4 Answers to self-assessment questions

(See 2.2 above)

1 Client dissatisfaction is disappointment of the client in the goods or services being offered by an organisation. With most goods which are in competitive demand, client dissatisfaction can be relieved on a subsequent occasion by choosing goods made by another supplier – we simply do not go into that shop again once the present problem is sorted out. In other organisations where a monopoly exists or where the service is operated as a public service, and customers have no alternative to using the same organisation, client dissatisfaction can mount with each repetition of the frustrating situation.
2 Charismatic authority is authority derived from the charisma (gift of grace) of an outstanding individual or leader, whose personality commands obedience either by its innate qualities or because he/she has pursued policies which are manifestly better than those advocated by other institutions or organisations.
3 Traditional authority (the authority of chieftains) stems from an original authority of the charismatic type, passed on to descendants or heirs. In government it is the authority of monarchs; in business it is the authority of the family firm, run on patriarchal lines.

4  Legal authority is authority drawn from a procedural process. It may be fully legal, where authority is conferred by appointment of the sovereign body – for example, by Act of Parliament – or it may be purely procedural, as where a club or society, or the board of directors of a company, passes a resolution which is minuted and becomes part of 'standing orders' or a rule book. With legal authority, people are appointed to offices, and draw their authority from the tenure of the office.

5  Having been appointed to this particular office, I have certain duties to perform and will have a clear authority to give instructions and orders to a particular group of employees in the field specified. On the other hand, there will be higher-level staff above me, to whom I will report and to whom I will look for guidance if it appears that some matter is outside my own terms of reference or discretion. I shall also have duties which reach across from my own particular function into other areas where I shall be required to cooperate with other staff of the same general level as myself to advance the achievement of the objectives of the company and place my exporting expertise at the service of anyone requiring it.

6  Objectives will be defined by (a) the proprietor, if it is a sole trader business, or (b) the partners, or (c) the board of directors of a company or other organisation.

7  Objectives will be promulgated either directly by the managing director to the departmental managers or formally in a document such as a code of practice, manual of procedures, and so on.

8  Applicants would require (a) an application form; (b) a job description giving the exact requirements for the post, its probable duties and responsibilities; and (c) a background information sheet giving details of the company's history, interests, and so on.

9  Line organisations are those that have a direct line of authority from top to bottom, with each rank superior to its subordinates, in military style. A functional organisation is one where each area of activity, such as production, marketing, business administration, and so on, has its own status, and its own subsystems, so that it is in fact a number of line organisations cooperating together to achieve the objectives of the organisation.

10 The basic features of a multidivisional company are that it is split into a number of companies, each of which is a division of the group and largely autonomous under a chief executive whose function is to grow the division to achieve a sound return on the capital assets and other resources placed at his/her disposal. While cooperation with other divisions is expected it is not essential. The board exercises a general control over all divisions. There are several layers of management in each division which feed instructions down to the grass roots and feed comments, statistical returns, and so on, up the line to keep top management informed.

11 The basic features of an entrepreneurial company are an emphasis on innovation, a much reduced middle management and a greater awareness of the worth of all personnel. The mission statement drawn up by the leaders of the company sets the tone for the entire operations of the company, and the strategy statement that accompanies it sets out the proposed developments in the short and medium term. Everyone is expected to act generally in the interests of the company as a whole. New ideas result in the formation of new companies within the group, based on careful budgeting. Mentors and specialist advisers guide and encourage each new project.

12 Loop controls are control systems which feed back information to modify a subsystem in the light of defects revealed by its outputs, so that the subsystem achieves more perfectly the aims for which it was established. They may be direct loops of the type described, or more sophisticated loops which change the goals to be achieved by the subsystem in view of the new situation revealed by the information available.

## 2.5   Examination questions

1   What is meant by the term 'the structure of an organisation'? How is such a structure established? Refer in your answer to organisations of which you have personal experience, wherever possible.

2   Draw up a list of three personalities in modern life whom you would regard as charismatic. Explain the charismatic qualities of one of them in detail.

3   'Bureaucratic organisation dominates modern society, because of its greater technical efficiency.' Describe bureaucratic organisation and comment on its efficiency today.

4   Mr A is a relatively junior member of staff in the training department of Industrial Chemicals Corporation. How will he achieve promotion in such an organisation? In your answer comment on the problems facing such an individual in achieving his personal aims in a framework of bureaucratic organisation.

5   Businessman to youth employment officer: 'I need a really unintelligent person for this job in my garment factory, but after training the pay is good.' Why might an employer seek such an individual? What advantage might he/she achieve from employing less intelligent staff in some positions?

6   Explain the term 'systems approach' when thinking about an organisation. Why is a manager who adopts this approach likely to produce better results than one who is preoccupied with his own particular sector of activity in a large and complex organisation?

7   What is the relationship between the environment in which an organisation seeks to flourish and the system set up by its management team?

8   In the 1980s and 1990s the multidivisional company faced serious difficulties. What is a multidivisional company and why did it face difficulties in the closing years of the twentieth century?

9   'Around the world 32 726 Innovation Group employees are moving towards growth and prosperity. They are a diverse group, and each one is unique. They are pooling their talents and energies to serve our customers world-wide.' What sort of company is Innovation Group, do you suppose? Outline the nature of such companies.

10 What is 'empowerment'? How does empowerment release the energies and enterprise of staff previously thought of as 'low-level'? How is supervision exercised when there are no supervisors?

11 What is meant by a 'loop' control system? Distinguish between open loops and closed loops. Illustrate your answer from any situation you have experienced or read about, where such controls are used.
(For a suggested answer to this question see below)

## 2.6    Study tips: guide to the answer to question 11

1    First we need an explanation of 'loop' control systems. Something like:
     'Loop' control is a method of gaining control over a system such as a manufacturing system or a social programme, by monitoring it to discover changes that are manifesting themselves. The method leads to a feedback of information to interested parties and calls for responses to the information in the form of adjustments to the system. Thus a change in acidity or alkalinity in a manufacturing process might call for adjustment to the inputs, temperatures, pressures, and so on. A social programme going over budget would need to be cut back, or economies would need to be made, or an increased budget provided.

2    Open loops are loops where some human interference is called for, and this may be at a variety of levels. It could be at operative level, where an operator takes steps to adjust the system in some way in view of the adverse trend developing. It could be at a planning level, with a revision of plans resulting from the observed departure of actual results from anticipated results. It could be at board level, with a major policy review required.

3    A closed loop is one where human intervention is not required and the process of correcting the observed changes is purely automatic. Thus if falling temperatures close a thermostat to restart a heating process, or increased alkalinity causes the addition of acid particles, or declining oxygen level indications are corrected by the release of oxygen into the system, it is a closed loop.

4    Marks would be given for relevant illustrations and ideas from the student's own experience.

# 3 The structure of business enterprise

## 3.1 Revision test: structures of business enterprises

(To consolidate your knowledge of Chapter 3 in the main text)

| Answers | Questions |
| --- | --- |
| | 1 What are the chief types of private enterprise unit? |
| 1 Sole traders, partnerships, private limited companies and public limited companies. | 2 Why are many businesses still run as sole traders? |
| 2 For the following reasons:<br>(a) small markets – will only support a small business<br>(b) independence – many sole traders prefer to be free of control. | 3 What are the advantages of partnership? |
| 3 (a) Extra capital for development;<br>(b) mutual support – in sickness and for ordinary purposes like holidays<br>(c) extra experience and knowledge<br>(d) combination of experience and youthful energy. | 4 Why do many small firms set up as private limited companies? |
| 4 In order to gain the privilege of limited liability. | 5 What is the advantage of limited liability? |
| 5 The business is a separate legal personality from the owners of the business, who consequently can lose only the money they have invested in the firm – the issued capital. Their personal property cannot be claimed by any creditors. | 6 What are the outstanding features of a public limited liability company? |
| 6 (a) The shares can be bought and sold publicly on stock exchanges<br>(b) as very large sums of capital can be collected in this way the enterprises can be on a very large scale. | 7 What are the chief types of non-profit-making organisation? |
| 7 Clubs and cooperative societies. | 8 What are the chief public enterprise business units? |
| 8(a) Autonomous corporations<br>(b) nationalised industries;<br>(c) government departments<br>(d) local government departments. | 9 What is a quango? |

| Answers | Questions |
| --- | --- |
| 9 A quasi-autonomous non-governmental organisation. | **10 What does quasi mean?** |
| 10 Almost. Quangos are almost autonomous, but governments can question what they are doing, and perhaps refuse to fund what the quango proposes. | **11 Where are quangos used?** |
| 11 In many situations where ministers are not sure what is the best policy to pursue, and they appoint a quango of knowledgeable people to bring forward clear proposals. | **12 Go over the questions again until you are sure of the answers Then try the exercises below.** |

## 3.2   Self-assessment questions

(Answers on p. 17)

Here are nine questions about Chapter 3 in the main text. Take a sheet of paper and do what is required in each case. Then go through the self-assessment procedure for each question and give yourself a mark out of 100. File these sheets for revision later.

1  What is an entrepreneur?
2  What are the requirements for setting up a sole trader business?
3  What are the advantages and disadvantages of setting up in partnership?
4  Explain the principle of limited liability.
5  What information has to be given when registering a company?
6  What is a producer cooperative?
7  How would you justify the establishment of the Atomic Energy Authority as a nationalised institution?
8  What is a holding company?
9  What is a quango?

## 3.3   A project on your local business area

In this chapter we have been studying the types of business unit to be found in a mixed economy such as the UK. To study these units in your own home area, take your local shopping centre (if it is big enough) or if necessary a section of the shopping area in your nearest town. Take only one side of the main high street for a distance of about 150 metres in a very busy area, or 250 metres in a less busy area. Write down the name of each business outlet in that stretch of road and whether it seems to be a sole trader, a partnership, a private limited company, and so on.

Business people are often secretive about their affairs and may be unwilling to reveal their true business situation, so if you are asked make it clear that you are only carrying out an assignment for educational purposes. There may well be several outlets which you cannot identify clearly. Draw up a report on the types of business and the number of each type in the area chosen.

# 3.4   Answers to self-assessment questions

(See section 3.2 above)

1  An entrepreneur is a person who shows enterprise, undertaking to create the goods and services required by humankind by assuming an organisation role in their provision, distribution and supply to the general public.

2  There are no requirements to set up a sole trader organisation other than the display of a business name which is either the true name of the owner or, if it is an invented name, shows who the true proprietor is, for example 'Vegetarian Foods (proprietor D. Smith)'.

3  The advantages are:
   a mutual support in times of sickness, holidays, and so on
   b increased capital
   c wider experience – 'two heads are better than one'
   d privacy of affairs.
The disadvantages are:
   a unlimited liability
   b death or retirement brings the firm to an end
   c profits must be shared
   d decisions have to be mutually agreed, which may cause delay.

4  The principle of limited liability is that a person who has contributed capital to an organisation does not thereby assume full responsibility for all the actions of the firm or company and is not legally liable for either its debts or its torts (civil wrongs). The liability of the investor is limited to the amount of capital contributed, and no further, so the investor can lose what is put into the business, but is not liable to have other assets such as a home, a car, and so on, seized and sold to pay any debts of the business.

5  When registering a company the promoters draw up a Memorandum of Association which includes seven main points:
   a the name of the company ending in Ltd or PLC
   b the address
   c the objects clause
   d a statement that the liability of the shareholders is limited
   e the amount and types of capital
   f an undertaking by the signatories that they desire to be formed into a registered company, and
   g the names and addresses of the first director (or directors) and the first company secretary.

6  A producer cooperative is a cooperative registered either under the Friendly Societies Act or as a company limited by guarantee (not shares) whose members work together in some enterprise which they deem to be socially beneficial, or mutually profitable. There is no transferable equity capital and the members act as both directors and employees.

7  We could advance the following reasons:
   a nuclear energy is a very dangerous industry and the only safe control is a centralised official authority

   b close adherence to safety guidelines is essential and efficient monitoring of this aspect would in any case be necessary

   c nuclear energy is a natural resource, and should be nationally owned

   d experience in the USA of privately owned nuclear plants does not encourage confidence in them

   e if anything goes wrong, only the nation is big enough to pick up the bill for putting things right.

8 A holding company is one which has over 50 percent of the shares of another company (or companies) and therefore has control of them and 'holds' them in its power. As a result a holding company is called a group, and the companies held are called subsidiaries. If it has less than 50 percent but still has a considerable holding, they are called associated companies.

9 A quango is a quasi-autonomous non-governmental organisation. They are set up to supervise various aspects of business and social activity (for example, in the United Kingdom the Central Transport Consultative Committee is influential in all aspects of transport and distribution).

## 3.5   Examination questions

1 List the common types of business organisation, dividing your list into:
   a private sector and
   b public sector units.

2 Why may a sole trader find it necessary to take a partner? What are the disadvantages of doing so?

3 Who provides the capital for each of the organisations listed below? Who is entitled to any profits made? Give your answers in tabular form.
   a Sole trader
   b Partnerships
   c Limited companies
   d Cooperative societies
   e The Department of Health
   f The Atomic Energy Authority
   g A municipal council
   h The House of Lords

4 What is meant by limited liability? Why has the limited liability company become such an important form of organisation in free enterprise and mixed economies all over the world?

5 How is a private company formed?

6 What considerations have led to the privatisation of most of the formerly nationalised industries in the United Kingdom? Refer in your answer to several typical industries.

7 You are considering taking up a post in junior management. Two jobs appeal to you. One is in the retail field, as manager of a branch shop. The other is in a public service

office in the social security field. Outline the likely activities you would need to supervise in these rather different fields.

8 You have decided to go into business with a friend to exploit an invention which you have developed jointly. Consider what form of business you should set up and say why. What initial problems would you need to overcome? (See 3.6 for a suggested answer to this question.)

9 A quango has been appointed by the Minister for Energy to advise about nuclear power. It has representatives of the government, the industry and members of the public, some from the environmental lobby. What are the advantages and disadvantages of such a body?

## 3.6 Study tips: guide to the answer to question 8

1 The obvious forms of business unit are the partnership and the private limited company. The trouble is that all new businesses face quite serious financial problems and since partners are liable to the limit of their personal wealth for the losses of the business it is better to pick the limited company form where liability is limited to the amount of capital contributed. Even then it may not be possible to borrow money from banks or finance houses without giving a personal guarantee, but the fact that one is liable to one or two secured creditors is less worrying than being liable to every single creditor who supplies the business with equipment or materials.

2 The initial problems that need to be overcome include:
   a A decision about premises, which may include planning permission, meeting certain standards for the Factory Acts and Health and Safety legislation, and so on.
   b A decision about equipment, plant and machinery, and so on.
   c A decision about staffing. Is it necessary to take on staff and can we get people with the right skills and qualifications?
   d A decision about finance. We must draw up careful costings and budgets for the first year or more, and try to calculate a break-even point at which we will recover our costs and move into profit.
   e It is wise to divide the work envisaged so that each has his/her area of responsibility.
   f The company must be registered or, if we are buying an off-the-shelf company, we must send in the details to change the registration to our own name, and so on.
   g It is important to register for VAT if living in the UK, unless turnover is expected to be less than the minimum figure at the time. Even then we may want to register voluntarily.

# 4    The production function

## 4.1    Revision test: production

(To consolidate your knowledge of Chapter 4 in the main text)

| Answers | Questions |
|---|---|
| | **1 What is the purpose of production?** |
| 1 To create utilities which will satisfy wants. | **2 What are the resource requirements of any production system?** |
| 2 You need raw materials (provided by nature) and components (semi-manufactured goods) plus labour appropriate to the tasks to be performed and capital (a stock of assets, land, buildings, machinery, and so on). | **3 What are the chief types of production?** |
| 3 Job production (unit production); batch production; flow production; and process production. | **4 What is the chief feature of job production?** |
| 4 It is a one-off activity – we have to make a specific item and the job must carry the complete costs incurred, since there is no chance of spreading the costs over repeat orders. | **5 What is batch production?** |
| 5 It is production of a reasonable number of similar items which we know will be needed. The batch can be stored until required and costs can be spread across the whole batch. | **6 What is flow production?** |
| 6 It is mass production by continuous working methods in which work-in-progress flows through the factory in a steady stream to become a finished product. | **7 What is process production?** |
| 7 It is a system of production where a natural resource moves through a series of processes to become eventually a more useful product, with perhaps a number of by-products along the way. | **8 What are the chief activities in production administration?** |
| 8 Production engineering, production planning and production control. | **9 What is production engineering?** |
| 9 It is the technical side of production, in which jobs are analysed for their material content, their process implications – which vary from industry to industry – | *(continues overleaf)* |

| Answers | Questions |
|---|---|
| the jigs and specialist tools required, and so on. There is always a costing problem with this type of job evaluation, so material costs, labour costs and overheads enter into the decisions made. | **10 What is production planning?** |
| 10 It is the process of fitting a new job into the present production system, evaluating the job itself, estimating and quoting for it, preparing drawings, materials schedules, machine loadings, and so on, and issuing works orders to start the job up. | **11 What is production control?** |
| 11 It has three elements: material control, progress control (in which the progress of components and parts is chased to ensure there are no bottlenecks in production) and quality control (in which samples of end-product are analysed or examined to ensure correct quality). | **12 What is critical path analysis?** |
| 12 A technique which examines the implementation of any major programme to decide which activity must be carried out first and how other activities then follow and in what sequence. | **13 What is the 'critical path'?** |
| 13 It is the sequence of main events that lead from one vital event to another and eventually brings the project to completion. Other non-vital events can be got ready to play their part so long as they are completed by their own deadline and do not hold up the main work. | **14 Why is costing important in production?** |
| 14 Because we live in a competitive world and we must be able to quote prices which are competitive but still leave us enough when all expenses are paid to yield a profit at the end. | **15 What are the chief costing methods?** |
| 15 Job costing, contract costing, process costing, absorption costing, marginal costing and standard costing. | **16 What is a 'make or buy' decision?** |
| 16 One which appraises a new job to decide whether we can make it with existing capacity or need to buy it in from another firm at the best price possible. | **17 What are the two elements of work study?** |
| 17 Method study and work measurement. | **18 What is CAD?** |
| 18 Computer-aided design. The computer is used to draw technical diagrams and prepare schedules of material usage, parts and components. It also simulates production activities so that working procedures can be devised and tested on screen, and snags found before production even begins. | **19 What is CAM?** |
| 19 Computer-aided manufacturing. The production activities are computer controlled, usually with an endless band of tape which instructs the machines to produce a part or component time after time after time. | **20 What is CIM?** |

| Answers | Questions |
|---|---|

20 Computer-integrated manufacture. Here the fullest use of computerised techniques is employed to perform complex manufacturing processes using robotic layouts to manufacture, inspect and pass components and assemblies.

**21 Go over the questions again until you are sure of all the answers. Then try the self-assessment questions below.**

## 4.2    Self-assessment questions

(Answers on p. 24)

Here are 11 questions about Chapter 4 in the main text. Take a sheet of paper and do what is required in each case. Then go through the self-assessment procedure for each question and give yourself a mark out of 100. File these sheets for revision later.

1   In broad terms, what considerations affect the production policy of a firm?
2   Explain 'job production' and 'batch production'.
3   What considerations enter into the selection of a site for a factory?
4   A member of the middle management team is designated 'plant and equipment assessor'. What sort of things might he/she do under this designation?
5   What would you consider are the 'design implications' of producing a new product?
6   Distinguish between an estimate and a quotation.
7   Explain the terms (a) 'sequence schedule' and (b) 'loading programme' in production planning.
8   What is the importance of marginal costing in 'make or buy' decisions?
9   Explain the two aspects of work study.
10 What is network analysis?
11 Explain the terms 'event', 'activity' and 'duration time' in network analysis.

## 4.3    A project on production

Below are nineteen products produced around the world. There is a space for a twentieth one in case you have worked in production at some time and would like to do your project on a product you know a lot about. What we need is a small portfolio about one of these twenty products. It will tell us the following things (in so far as you can discover them from encyclopedias, the Internet or any other source).

a   What the product is and who needs it?
b   What is it made from and what is the source of its raw materials?
c   What type of production is used in making it? Is it capital intensive or labour intensive? What costs are incurred?

d How is it marketed? Remember a thing is not finally produced until it reaches the Final consumer, who wants to be satisfied.

The products are:

| | |
|---|---|
| 1 wheat | 11 lap-top computer |
| 2 car tyres | 12 petrol (gasoline) |
| 3 leather handbags | 13 cutlery |
| 4 cocoa | 14 milk |
| 5 a computer printer | 15 rubber |
| 6 a C.D. | 16 a super-sonic aircraft |
| 7 a padlock | 17 a two-inch nail |
| 8 copper | 18 cement |
| 9 a television set | 19 beachwear |
| 10 designer fashions | 20 . . . . . . . . . . (your own choice) |

# 4.4 Answers to self-assessment questions

(See 4.2 above)

1 The chief considerations are the nature of the product; its design, material content and packaging; the volume of output required; the techniques necessary; and the control procedures required.

2 Job production is production of a one-off, bespoke order for a customer. Each job has to be evaluated and the price must reflect the cost of all jigs, tools, and so on that are necessary. Batch production is production of a number of units, not necessarily required at once but certain to be needed in the future, for example 15 000 television control knobs. The surplus must be stored and issued as required against requisitions. As these are used up, a further batch will be manufactured.

3 The chief considerations are closeness to raw materials, or the port of import for foreign materials, closeness to a means of transport, closeness to a source of power, closeness to the market, closeness to a source of specialised labour or unskilled labour. Other factors include the availability to expand in the future without relocation – in other words, a site must be big enough to permit growth.

4 A person is usually appointed to keep a watching brief on all technical developments in a firm's particular field, especially, for example, any developments in the application of computers to production. Such a person receives all the trade journals that are issued, visits all relevant exhibitions and displays, perhaps purchases and evaluates new devices and makes recommendations about their adoption, and so on.

5 Every new product brings two sets of design problems. First there is the design of the product itself, its shape, construction, materials, range of sizes, and so on. Then there is the need with many products to design production facilities which will enable it to be mass-produced. We may need special tools, presses, and so on, and jigs of various sorts.

A jig is a device which holds a piece of equipment and guides tools onto it so that each piece does not have to be dealt with individually but can be quickly placed into a correct position where it can be drilled, planed, ground, and so on, easily and quickly.

6  An estimate is a rough price which can serve as a guideline to a customer considering placing an order. A quotation is an exact price offer which is susceptible to immediate acceptance to make a binding contract. An estimate can be revised later to take account of the actual cost of production; a quotation is a clear offer which, if accepted unequivocally, becomes a binding contract.

7  a  A sequence schedule is a list of processes which a part must pass through before it becomes a finished job. The schedule becomes a route card which controls the movement of the part through the various cost centres, until completion, testing and packaging.

   b  A loading programme is a record kept for machines to show how they are loaded with unfulfilled work. As jobs are completed they are removed from the loading record and further orders can be allocated to the machine. Delivery times must be gauged according to the loading and any breakdown affecting delivery time should be notified to the customer as soon as possible.

8  In a 'make or buy' decision the cost of making the product is always judged on the marginal costs only, that is, the extra costs involved if we make the product. There is no point allocating any charge for fixed overheads, since the fixed costs have already been incurred and taking the extra job will not add to them. It is only the variable costs that matter. Any outsider offering to supply has to do so at a price less than our marginal costs, otherwise we might as well make the item ourselves.

9  The two aspects of work study are method study and work measurement. Method study analyses the work to be done and decides on the best and most economical way of doing it commensurate with the quality required. Work measurement seeks to discover a standard cost for doing that class of work, using the method prescribed by the method study engineers. This standard cost then enters into both the wages of employees and the pricing of the job to the customer.

10 Network analysis is a technique for planning a complex series of events so that they reach fruition in the shortest possible time. By a process of critical path analysis in which activities and events are set down on paper to show the durations of each activity leading into each event, we can find the longest series of activities. We plan these to proceed one after the other, with shorter contributing activities planned to fit in so that they do not delay any part of the critical path. (Study Fig. 4.2 again if necessary.)

11 An 'event' is a happening (such as the start-up procedure or the completion of a component). An 'activity' is a procedure leading up to an event. A 'duration time' is the time it takes to complete an activity. No event is reached until all the activities leading into it have been completed, and no activity can start until the event it starts from, the tail event, has been reached.

# 4.5    Examination questions

1   What do you consider to be the most important factors in the management of the system of production in a business?
2   Explain the term 'preventive maintenance'. What information would be necessary in an engineering group in order to set up a schedule of preventive maintenance? In your answer refer to daily, monthly and annual inspections. (See below for a suggested answer to this question.)
3   What is 'material flow' in a production organisation? Explain why it should be considered carefully.
4   What is a 'make or buy' decision? A manufacturer of small electrical appliances is debating whether to make or buy a component used in one appliance. What considerations enter into the decision and what are the advantages and disadvantages of each method?
5   What is method study? Outline a procedure for examining and reporting on, and then improving, an area of activity in either production or distribution.
6   Your managing director has asked you to recommend a site for a new factory. What criteria would you consider in making your suggestions?
7   What is supervision? What factors make supervision effective?
8   'Computerisation will cause redundancies.' 'Only computerisation can create increased employment opportunities in this industry.' Are these two views expressed about the same manufacturing industry incompatible with one another? In your answer draw on your own knowledge and experience of the impact of computerisation wherever possible.
9   What is meant by 'work study'? Explain how you would introduce work study into your organisation and the benefits you would hope to achieve by this change in working practice.
10 Quality control is an essential element in any manufacturing process. What are the essential features of quality control? In what ways can quality be controlled in situations such as (a) the manufacture of nails and (b) the manufacture of artistic pots?
11 Discuss the part played by materials handling in manufacturing enterprises. Why should this area be the subject of regular review by management?

# 4.6    Study tips: guide to the answer to question 2

1   We need a definition. Something like:
    Preventive maintenance, as its name implies, is a system of regular maintenance and overhaul designed to prevent breakdowns – particularly plant failures, though it applies to every type of facility, such as buildings, roadways, plant access points, machines of all types, and so on. Any unexpected failure can be costly in idle time for operatives, penalty clauses in contracts, missed opportunities in selling, and so on.

Preventive maintenance seeks to anticipate breakdowns and provide reserves of spare parts and so on for emergency repairs.

2   The sort of things we require are:

a A detailed inventory of plant, listing its location, component units, likely failure points, spare parts required, working life, breakdown history, running maintenance required.

b This should enable us to draw up maintenance schedules for inspection, routine replacement of parts liable to failure, appoint suitably qualified staff if necessary or make firm arrangements for prompt service if outside contractors have to be used.

c Clear manuals of procedure should be written which not only form the basis of training and routine procedures but are available for consultation in emergency. They should include names, addresses, telephone and fax numbers of specialist contractors who may be required.

3   In general, maintenance fits into a regular pattern:

a The daily round should include certain routine procedures, lubrication, inspection for visible defects, overheating, leaking, and so on. The importance of reporting unusual developments should be stressed, and a record card, requiring signature by each shift operative, with a Remarks column, should be available. Defect report cards should be available at all times – with a known authority to whom they are to be passed.

b A regular, more formal, inspection should be agreed at specified times – it could be monthly but some other guideline, 6000 miles for vehicles or 100 hours running for machines, might be more suitable. A list of points to be checked and inspected should be available.

c For some things (buildings, for example), an annual (or six-monthly) review should be held at a reasonably high level.

# 5  The purchasing function

## 5.1  Revision test: purchasing

(To consolidate your knowledge of Chapter 5 in the main text)

| Answers | Questions |
| --- | --- |
| | 1 What is the function of the purchasing department (or buying department)? |
| 1 To obtain for the firm all its resource requirements, except labour (which is found by the personnel department). | 2 What are the four chief types of requirement? |
| 2 (a) Capital assets<br>(b) consumable items<br>(c) goods for resale<br>(d) raw materials and components if the firm is a manufacturing enterprise. | 3 How could a production department with a new product to make initiate the necessary supplies? |
| 3 By drawing up a specification of requirements for the new product, capital items, raw materials and components so that the purchasing department can start to seek the necessary supplies. | 4 What is an index of suppliers? |
| 4 It is a list of approved suppliers with whom the purchasing department has had the necessary consultations and has drawn up contractual agreements for the supply of particular types of materials, goods or capital items which meet the firm's requirements as to quality, quantity and price. | 5 What arrangements will the purchasing department make before orders are placed with a supplier? |
| 5 Generally speaking, apart from introductory orders to assess the quality of a supplier's goods or services, the purchasing officer will not place orders with a supplier until preliminary discussions have taken place and, wherever possible, clear contractual terms have been agreed between the parties. These terms will form the agreed basis for all future dealings. | 6 What are the advantages of centralised buying? |
| 6 (a) Only officially authorised staff may place orders for the firm or company.<br>(b) A multiplicity of small departmental orders is avoided and bulk orders, commanding bulk discounts, are placed by head office.<br>(c) Prices, delivery terms, and so on, will be centrally negotiated and suitable credit periods arranged. | 7 Go through the sequence of events when ordering goods from a supplier. |

| Answers | Questions |
|---|---|
| 7 (a) Check that the requisitioned goods are not in stock. (b) If so, check that the requisition is signed by an approved person. (c) Find the usual supplier, or one of the usual suppliers. (d) If it seems advisable, telephone to check the availability of the item and warn that an order will follow. (e) Make out the official order, giving all relevant details and get it signed by the purchasing officer before sending. (f) Chase the progress of the order if it fails to arrive in the normal re-order time. | **8 Go through the procedure for receiving goods.** |
| 8 (a) Inspect the goods on arrival. (b) If they seem all right, give a guarded clean signature (e.g. 'Received in apparent good order'). (c) Unpack goods and compare with advice note. (d) Make out a goods received note and use it to update stock records, or bin card. (e) Send copies to purchasing department and notify requisitioning department of availability of item. | **9 What is inventory control?** |
| 9 It is the control of stocks and capital items to ensure that losses due to pilfering, misappropriation, wastage and so on, are avoided so far as is possible. | **10 What is the rate of stock turnover?** |
| 10 It is a ratio calculated to show how many times the average stock turns over in the year. | **11 What is the formula for it?** |
| 11 Rate of stock-turn = Cost of stock sold / Average stock at cost price | **12 What is the gross profit percentage?** |
| 12 It is a ratio which tells us what percentage of total sales our gross profit is. If the gross profit percentage falls from one trading period to another, it means that something has happened to our arrangements that needs investigating. It may be the sales figure is lower (staff stealing the takings) or the stock figure is lower (shoplifting or misappropriation of stock). There may of course be a perfectly understandable reason for the fall. | **13 What is the formula for gross profit percentage?** |
| 13 Gross profit x 100 / Turnover | **14 What is an EOQ?** |
| 14 It is the economic order quantity for purchasing a particular item of stock. It is that volume of stock which incurs the minimum total cost in re-order charges and holding charges (see Fig. 5.4 in the main text). | **15 Go over the questions again until you are sure of all the answers. Then try the self-assessment exercises which follow.** |

## 5.2   Self-assessment questions

(Answers on p. 30)

Here are eight questions about Chapter 5 in the main text. Take a sheet of paper and do what is required in each case. Then go through the self-assessment procedure for each question and give yourself a mark out of 100. File these sheets for revision later.

1   What is the function of the purchasing department?
2   What are the duties of the purchasing officer?
3   To which professional body would a purchasing officer usually belong?
4   Outline the procedure for drawing up an index of suppliers.
5   A delivery vehicle arrives and the driver asks you to sign the delivery note. What is your reaction to this request?
6   What exactly is a requisition?
7   Explain the procedure for ordering and receiving supplies.
8   Explain the terms (a) re-order level and (b) economic order quantity.

## 5.3   A project on purchasing

Below are the names of four new companies each giving a strong clue as to the types of trade they intend to carry on. Choose any one of them and consider the types of supplies they will require.

a   The Mediterranean Toppings Pizza Co Ltd
b   Specialist Garden Supplies (Furniture) Ltd
c   Beech-block Flooring Ltd
d   Security Electrical Alarms (Cambridge) Ltd

Draw up a form for completion by prospective suppliers in which they are invited to give details of their goods and services. The proprietors of the company you have chosen wish to know (among other things that will come to your mind) the following points:

a   Full details of the name, address, etc of the proposed supplier, including a contact to whom the customer requiring supplies should apply.
b   Their terms of trade, including credit period allowed (if any), and details of the finance provided for capital items if purchased on hire purchase etc.
c   Delivery arrangements for regular orders, and any discounts available.
d   We would like to see a catalogue, if available, or any leaflets about products.
e   Make it clear that this is only a preliminary enquiry and cannot be turned into an order of any sort until more detailed negotiations have taken place.

It may be that you will prefer to draw up different forms for use when enquiring about (a) Capital items (b) trade goods and (c) consumables, including office products.

You may find your local *Yellow Pages* a good source of ideas for what to include on your form(s).

# 5.4    Answers to self-assessment questions

1   The function of the purchasing department is to obtain for the firm or company all its resource requirements (except labour) at the best price possible, consistent with the quality of materials, components, and so on, required. It offers a body of expertise in buying to all other departments, replacing what would otherwise be a rather haphazard process by a professional purchasing system, buying from approved suppliers who have been made aware of the firm's needs.

2   The duties of the purchasing officer are to build up an index of approved suppliers, with whom sound contracts have been made for the supply of goods as and when required, upon known standard terms and conditions. He/she will then consider requisitions from authorised staff and turn them into valid orders, clearly specifying what is required. The resulting goods will be checked on arrival, entered as 'goods received' in the stores records and issued to the requisitioning department. All shortages or claims will be pursued before the account is settled.

3   A purchasing officer would usually be a corporate member or fellow of the Chartered Institute of Purchasing and Supply.

4   To draw up an index of suppliers we must:
    a find suppliers who usually supply goods of the type we require
    b acquaint them with our particular needs, giving detailed specifications, and ask them to quote prices for future delivery if accepted as suitable suppliers. We may also ask for specimen items if this is appropriate
    c if the responses to (b) seem to augur well we should approach them formally to discuss contractual terms for future supplies, in the volumes likely to be required. We might seek assurances of goodwill and intention to supply on a 'favoured customer' basis to impress on them the importance to our operations of orders placed with them
    d if this is satisfactory we should add them to our list as approved suppliers and then place orders as regularly as possible to cement the relationship.

5   Generally speaking, I would be hesitant. There may be someone who is authorised to receive goods and to sign delivery notes. If I do not know how to assess the quality or quantity being delivered I would not sign, but I would try to find the appropriate reception clerk. If no-one else was about and the package appeared intact I would give a claused signature, 'Received in apparent good order, but unopened.'

6   A requisition is a request to be supplied with an item needed for production. It may be for a quantity of material, or a component, or a supply of some consumable material such as a pad of forms or a packet of continuous stationery, or it may be for a tool, piece of equipment, and so on. If the item is in store it will be issued. If it is not, the requisition will be passed to the purchasing department who will order the item from an authorised supplier.

7   The procedure is:
    a check that the requisition is properly authorised by a competent person
    b find the authorised supplier or one of them

c if necessary check the availability of the item with the supplier

d produce an official order giving the full specification and referring to the usual contractual terms as applying

e when the goods arrive, check them before signing the delivery note and, if necessary, give notice of damage or delay

f make out a goods received note and enter the item into stock

g pass the goods received note to purchasing department and notify the requisitioning department of the availability of the item.

8 The re-order level is the level at which the storekeeper must order up a further supply of an item. Suppose it takes 3 weeks to deliver an item after ordering and the factory uses 80 per week. The number required in the replacement interval would be 240. This is therefore the minimum stock level and the re-order level would be slightly above this, say 300 items.

## 5.5 Examination questions

1 'The function of the purchasing officer is to secure such assets, raw materials, components and consumable materials as may be required by the organisation, as economically as possible.' How is this aim achieved?

2 What is meant by the term 'stores'? What is meant by the term 'stores control'? Mention in your answer the particular aspects of stores which need controlling and how supervision of them should be maintained.

3 Many retail outlets are supplied with stock by head offices on a daily basis, or a weekly basis, the branch being charged with the goods at selling price. What is the point of this technique? In your answer refer particularly to the question of inventory control and financial control.

4 Write short notes (5 to 8 lines) on the following aspects of purchasing:

a Approved suppliers

b Goods received notes

c Economic order quantities

d Payment of invoices for goods supplied

5 What are the essential principles of form design? Draw up a requisition to be used in a stores department for recording the requisitioning of loose tools. You need to know the name of the person requesting the loan, the job number, the period for which required, any special bits or parts required, the date of issue and the due date for return. The location of the job should be shown and the hourly/daily charge for costing purposes.

6 a Explain the relationship of the purchasing department to the other departments in a business.

b Draw up an order form showing the required details, inventing these for imaginary firms and any class of goods in which you are interested.

7  A buyer receives quotations from three suppliers, as follows:

| Trade discount (%) | Delivery | Terms of payment |
|---|---|---|
| A   15 | Immediate | One month net |
| B   40 | 3 months | 2.5% cash discount 30 days |
| C   55 | 14 days | Cash with order |

What factors would the buyer need to take into account before deciding which quotation to accept?

8  What considerations should be borne in mind when an order is about to be placed with a new supplier?

9  What is inventory control? Discuss the need for inventory control and the problems that have to be solved to achieve it.

# 5.6   Study tips: model answer to question 9

1  The question calls for a definition. It should be something along the following lines. 'Inventory control is the control of stocks, or stores, and also the control of capital items such as furniture, equipment, tools, and so on.'

2  A general discussion of the need for stocks and stores is then required; stocks are held to make production possible even though demand fluctuates. The aim is never to be out of stock but never to be over-stocked because that represents capital tied up to no useful purpose. With regard to inventories of capital items, the aim of inventory control is to check pilferage, breakages and other types of loss, review stocks for obsolescence, fair wear and tear, and so on, and assist the disposal of redundant items.

3  We now need some discussion of the measures needed to keep control of stocks, such as:

a  Specification of minimum stock levels and ways to avoid running out of stock – such as bagging up the minimum stock until a requisition for further supplies has been made out.

b  Specification of re-order levels to ensure replacement of low stocks.

c  Specification of EOQs (economic order quantities) taking account of average requirements, re-order periods, volume discounts, and so on.

4  Some discussion of stock-taking methods, perpetual inventory, spot-checks, and so on, would be appropriate.

# 6    The research and development function

## 6.1    Revision test: research and development

(To consolidate your knowledge of Chapter 6 in the main text)

| Answers | Questions |
|---|---|
| | 1 What is the function of the R&D department? |
| 1 To conduct research as and when required into all aspects of a company's work and organisation. | 2 What are the main research areas? |
| 2 They are (a) basic research<br>(b) problem-based research<br>(c) applied research<br>(d) development work in bringing an idea into full maturity as a new product or service which can be offered to customers. | 3 What is basic research? |
| 3 It is research in the general field of a company's interests, increasing the sum total of knowledge, without drive in any particular direction, but hoping that it may prove fruitful in the long run. It may also be sponsored officially, or by trade associations or industry-wide cooperatives. | 4 What is problem-based research? |
| 4 It is research aimed at solving particular problems, in products, services, packaging, distribution, administrative procedures, and so on. | 5 What are applied research and development? |
| 5 These are concerned with investigating and developing new ideas which will lead either to new products and services or to revamping of existing products and services to lengthen the lifetime of a product and meet competition. | 6 What are the stages of applied research and development? |
| 6 (a) The idea<br>(b) evaluation of the idea<br>(c) a feasibility study<br>(d) economic justification<br>(e) approval of the product<br>(f) a prototype, pilot plant, and so on<br>(g) full production<br>(h) launch of the new product. | 7 How can we generate ideas? |

| Answers | Questions |
|---|---|
| 7 (a) Outsiders approach us and we take up their suggestions for evaluation (b) internal staff are invited to submit suggestions in a 'suggestion box', with cash rewards (c) brainstorming. | **8 What is a patent, and how long does it last?** |
| 8 It is a government grant of exclusive privilege in making or selling a new invention which is capable of industrial application. It lasts 20 years. | **9 What is a trade mark, or a service mark?** |
| 9 They are names, logos or other devices which associate goods or services with some person, firm or company which has the right to use the mark. A registered mark gives an exclusive right to the proprietor to use the mark concerned. There might be many situations in which a firm or company would wish to register such a mark. | **10 Where does R&D fit into the business organisation?** |
| 10 It is a subsystem under the general span of control of a senior member of staff, such as the production manager or the marketing manager, but with links to all other departments who feed it with ideas and problems for solution. | **11 How may research costs be recovered?** |
| 11 (a) Out of the sale of new products and services if the idea comes to fruition (b) out of fees charged to outside bodies for consultancy services (c) out of an increase in charges made on all jobs done – an on-cost or overhead (d) if we cannot do that because a particular job is competitive, we load the charges made with what the contract will bear: no charge to competitive ones but higher charges to non-competitive contracts. | **12 Go over the questions again until you are sure of all the answers. Then try the self-assessment exercises below.** |

# 6.2   Self-assessment questions

(Answers on p. 35)

Here are eight questions about Chapter 6 in the main text. Take a sheet of paper and do what is required in each case. Then go through the self-assessment procedure for each question and give yourself a mark out of 100. File these sheets for revision later.

1   What are the four areas of R&D work?
2   Who conducts basic research?
3   How are ideas generated?
4   What is brainstorming?
5   Why might a company decide to patent a device developed in its R&D department?

6   Who owns the invention developed by a team of R&D staff in a major engineering company?

7   What is a service mark?

8   How may research costs be recovered?

## 6.3   A project on suggestion boxes

If you are at work there must be some aspect of your work that you feel dissatisfied with. Perhaps you feel at certain times that one aspect of your job is a tedious bore. Or again, one aspect may be more than you can manage and you feel a better system could be devised. If you are studying full time perhaps some aspect of your college year frustrates you in some way.

Your assignment is to submit a suggestion to a Suggestion Box outlining your ideas for resolving the problem. Go into the problem in as detailed a way as possible.

## 6.4   Answers to self-assessment questions

1   The four areas of R&D work are basic research, problem-based research, applied research and development work which seeks to turn an idea into a completed product or service which can be offered to customers.

2   Basic research may be conducted by any firm or company in its R&D department, but it is often organised as a cooperative effort by bodies such as trade associations. A great deal of basic research is carried out by government departments and research councils and also by non-departmental public bodies.

3   Ideas may be generated by outsiders (inventors and others who offer devices which may be of interest) or by insiders through a 'suggestions box' scheme. They may also contribute ideas at brainstorm sessions or after the deliberations of 'think tanks'.

4   Brainstorming is an attempt to generate new ideas by a meeting at which anyone may produce and argue in support of any idea, however outlandish. The idea is that no-one should be inhibited by the presence of superiors. All useful ideas are then considered more carefully and the best are selected for full investigation and development.

5   The products produced by an R&D department belong to the firm or company which employed the research team, and are the result of the team's duty to advance the employer's undertaking. To take full advantage of an invention it must be patented, otherwise a rival may pirate it and get the benefit of its exploitation. Once patented, the device may be marketed, or others may be allowed to produce it under license.

6   The invention is the property of the engineering company.

7   A service mark is a brand name or other device for a service which is being marketed by an individual, firm or company. If the mark ties the service to the proprietor, he/she may register it in the same way as a trade mark, and this gives exclusive use for seven

years. At the end of the seven years it may be renewed for a further 14 years, and after that for 14 years at a time, for as long as the proprietor wishes.

8  Research costs may be recovered:

a  out of the sale of any product that results or

b  out of the marketing of any service that results or

c  out of the sale of research papers, advice, and so on, or

d  from fees earned offering consultancy advice, or as expert witness at trials or arbitration proceedings and

e  from on-costs added to invoices (either all invoices issued or those invoices that can bear the costs without driving the customer elsewhere).

## 6.5    Examination questions

1  What is the purpose of the research and development department? Where does it fit into the business organisation scheme?

2  Discuss the merits of a 'suggestion box' scheme with cash rewards as a system for generating ideas. What procedures should be followed with suggestions made by employees?

3  It has been your company's practice to generate new ideas in-house so far as possible, and a small research and development team has been maintained for many years. A senior member of the team recently left and it is now discovered that he is working for a competitor, developing a project originally conceived in your company, where he was project leader. What course of action do you suggest? Explain the implications fully.

4  Under recent legislation in the United Kingdom it is possible to register a 'service' mark in the same way as a 'trade' mark. What are the advantages of such registrations?

5  In what ways may new ideas be generated for updating existing products and developing new ones? What sort of procedures could be adopted for screening and evaluating such ideas?

6  What is a patent? Why do we register patents and pursue through the courts those who infringe our patents? How do patents contribute to profitability?

7  What is 'problem-based research'? Suggest how such research might be tackled, by a medium-sized firm with fairly limited resources. You may illustrate your answer by reference to any typical problem either drawn from your own experience, or from the literature of a field you are familiar with, or an imaginary problem.

8  'The growing firm is at a disadvantage in research and development, and governments should be prepared to help.' What disadvantages face the small firm in this field and how may governments help?

9  What is the importance of basic research to a company offering scientific solutions to environmental problems? How should the costs of such research be recovered?

# 6.6   Study tips: suggested answer to question 9

1  *The importance of basic research* Here the student should make it clear that he/she understands basic research as being very broad-based research over the whole general field of scientific endeavour in the area under consideration (in this case environmental research). It is not research aimed at solving a particular problem (such as nitrogen run-off from agricultural areas), or research aimed at finding a use for waste products.

The importance of basic research in environmental matters is to advance humankind's general knowledge of ecosystems. It may lead nowhere, or it may lead to useful spin-offs which solve a known problem, or provide a marketable product. Unless a company engages in this type of research it will not keep up with its competitors or develop desirable skills which it can offer to customers with a problem.

2  *The recovery of the costs of basic research* This is a difficult problem. We may be able to recoup it as follows:

a By charging an overhead element on all jobs for customers which will reimburse us for the benefit the customer has received from our general enterprise.

b By charging a substantial contribution to jobs which can bear a charge, while ignoring such charges on jobs which are closely costed and cannot bear an extra charge without driving the customer elsewhere.

c By recouping the costs out of saleable products or services which result from the basic research carried out.

d By charging for literature embodying conclusions drawn from our research and marketed to professional and academic customers.

e By developing 'expert' services for use in legal and arbitration proceedings which will pay suitable fees for evidence pertaining to trials or disputes.

Students may think of other ideas which are worth marks.

# 7 The marketing function

## 7.1 Revision test: marketing 1

(To consolidate your knowledge of Chapter 7 in the main text)

| Answers | Questions |
|---|---|
| | 1 What is marketing? |
| 1 It is the activity which transfers finished goods from the point of production to the point of consumption, bridging the time gaps and the geographical gaps which separate producers from consumers, and effecting such changes of ownership of the goods as are necessary in the course of distribution, from manufacturer to wholesaler, or to retailer, or to final consumer, according to which channel of distribution is used. | 2 What is a marketing philosophy? |
| 2 It is the principle behind the marketing activities of a firm or company, which serves as a guiding light to sales, distribution and servicing staff. | 3 What is market research? |
| 3 It is investigation of a market to discover its total size, spending power, tastes and fashions. | 4 How may market research be carried out? |
| 4 By desk research; field research using postal surveys or interviews; or by studying market intelligence information made available by official bodies, trade associations, and so on. | 5 Why is public relations an important part of promotion? |
| 5 (a) Because in many cases it is free – the company is promoted because it, or its products are news, and there is no advertising charge<br>(b) even if the public relations is a negative activity (rebutting unfair criticism or allegations) a good PR performance may be very beneficial. | 6 What should the board of a company do to ensure sound public relations? |
| 6 Draw up and publish a PR policy in-house, so that everyone knows what the policy is and keeps within the limits set by the board. | 7 What would be the elements in such a PR policy? |
| 7 (a) The type of image the board is seeking to portray<br>(b) which sectors of the public they hope to influence favourably<br>(c) the importance of keeping the press officer fully informed so that he/she can represent the firm's position adequately<br>(d) the need for discretion when dealing with customers and suppliers. | 8 What are the duties of the head of publicity? |

| Answers | Questions |
|---|---|
| 8 (a) To draw up a programme of publicity balanced over the various media<br>(b) to build up a team of staff to handle all aspects of publicity<br>(c) to plan expenditure on a job-to-be-done basis and exercise budgetary control. | **9 What is the key phrase used by the Advertising Standards Authority?** |
| 9 Is the advertisement 'legal, decent, honest and truthful'? | **10 What are the chief media for advertising?** |
| 10 (a) The business press<br>(b) brochures<br>(c) exhibitions<br>(d) direct mail<br>(e) PR<br>(f) directories<br>(g) newspapers<br>(h) videos/audio-visuals<br>(i) point-of-sale assistance to traders<br>(j) posters<br>(k) sponsorship<br>(l) TV and radio<br>(m) the Internet. | **11 What is a break-even point?** |
| 11 It is that point at which the income from the sale of a product covers both the variable and the fixed costs, so that any further increase in sales will mean that a profit is made. | **12 How much profit will be made once the break-even point is passed?** |
| 12 An amount equal to the difference between the variable cost of the extra units and their selling price (the fixed costs having now been recovered anyway, the only costs to be recovered are those of the extra materials, labour and direct overheads). | **13 What is marginal costing?** |
| 13 It is a system of costing which says we need only study the additional costs (the marginal costs) arising from any order. So long as the price exceeds the marginal costs and we have spare capacity to produce the goods we might as well take the order and make what we can on it. | **14 What are the functions of the sales manager?** |
| 14 (a) To set up and control the sales office<br>(b) to appoint, induct, motivate and supervise a sales team<br>(c) to establish a sound documentation system for sales<br>(d) to co-operate in devising all advertising, special promotions, sales drives, and so on. | **15 How may a sales team be remunerated?** |
| 15 By (a) basic salary<br>(b) basic salary + commission<br>(c) basic salary + commission + bonuses at intervals. | **16 What basic principles apply to control a sales force?** |
| 16 (a) Allocate territories fairly<br>(b) clarify the procedure when a clash of sales means one salesman invades another's territory | *(continues overleaf)* |

| Answers | Questions |
|---|---|
| (c) provide a full range of stationery<br>(d) devise a report form for completion after every call made<br>(e) make the best use of sales conferences to expand knowledge of products, selling techniques, credit control procedures, and so on<br>(f) evaluate sales efforts on a regular basis. | **17 What is credit control?** |
| 17 It is a way of keeping control of firms and companies to whom we supply goods or services on credit, payable at a later date. | **18 What are the chief features of a credit control system?** |
| 18 (a) Never give credit to new customers; it is a privilege best earned by a probationary period<br>(b) always take up references on those who ask to become credit-worthy customers<br>(c) Make it clear how you expect customers to behave as far as payment is concerned. A set of 'Terms of trading' helps<br>(d) Always set a credit limit and do not go beyond it – insist on sticking to the rules. If necessary put them on pro-forma terms<br>(e) If they don't pay on time, ring them, followed by a formal request through your solicitor<br>(f) If necessary sue them (some people only pay those who are worrying them). | **19 Go over the test again until you are sure of all the answers. Then try the self-assessment questions below.** |

# 7.2    Self-assessment questions

(Answers at 7.4 below)

Here are eight questions about Chapter 7 in the main text. Take a sheet of paper and do what is required in each case. Then go through the self-assessment procedure for each question and give yourself a mark out of 100. File these sheets for revision later.

1  Define marketing, giving an explanation of what the marketing director seeks to do.
2  What is meant in marketing by 'bridging the gaps'?
3  What is 'a marketing philosophy'?
4  What is desk research?
5  What is 'public relations'?
6  What are the chief types of advertising?
7  What is meant by 'media' in the information industry?
8  What is a break-even point? What costs must be recovered before we can break even?

# 7.3 A project on marketing

Your project is to devise a set of stationery which will enable you to control a small sales force, each sales person having his/her own territory. Sales outside a territory may be pursued but commission on any such order will be shared equally with the other salesperson. The forms required are:

a A standard letter notifying firms that the representative will be calling on them at a date and time specified.

b A representative's report to be completed on the day of the visit and posted on to Head Office.

c A follow-up report notifying the representative of action taken on the matter reported in (b).

d An 'action this day' report on any special problem, complaint etc.

e A representative assessment report for a three-monthly review of operations.

# 7.4 Answers to self-assessment questions

(See 7.2 above)

1 Marketing is an activity that moves goods from the point of production across the time gaps and geographical gaps which separate producers from consumers, into the possession of another party who may be a wholesaler, a retailer or the final end-user, in such a way that a profit is achieved as a reward for the manufacturing and marketing effort involved. The marketing director's job is to co-ordinate all the various activities, market research, publicity, order processing, distribution, credit control, exporting, and so on, to achieve a profitable result after all these problems have been overcome.

2 Bridging the gaps is the process of bringing goods across two barriers. The first is the geographical divide that separates producers from consumers, and is achieved by transport and distribution procedures. The other gap is the time gap between production and consumption. During the time gap, goods may deteriorate, or be pilfered or stolen – problems which have to be overcome by merchandising skills appropriate to the class of goods concerned and by security measures.

3 A marketing philosophy is a set of principles which guide all members of staff in their day-to-day activities so that they create in the minds of suppliers, customers and all other business contacts a company image which is socially acceptable, equitable in all company dealings and reflects the goodwill borne to the company by the business community and the public at large.

4 Desk research is research based on in-house records, records provided by trade associations and published data available from official or commercial sources. It seeks to establish a sound understanding of the market for our products without conducting special enquiries by postal questionnaire or by interviewing.

5  Public relations is the procedure for establishing and maintaining an attractive public image by dealing with complaints sympathetically, bringing new developments to the public attention at the earliest possible date, rebutting adverse criticisms by forthright correction with the true facts and, if necessary, taking high-profile action to fight one's corner in any public debate or by legal action against slanderous or libellous statements.

6  The chief types of advertising are informative advertising – which seeks to inform the public about a product, its uses, advantages and disadvantages – and persuasive advertising – which seeks to persuade the public that a product is a better buy than comparable products, so as to increase market share.

7  The term 'media' has come to be used for any method of communication. Strictly speaking the word is the plural of 'medium', a word which in this context means a method by which ideas are communicated to individuals, groups or the public at large. The obvious media today are the press, radio and television, but there are many other methods of communication, for example direct mail, posters, free circulation magazines, exhibitions, directories, videos, and the Internet.

8  A break-even point is the point in a sales campaign where the income received from the sales exactly equals the total costs of production (the variable costs and the fixed costs). Every unit sold at a profit covers its variable costs and makes a 'contribution' over and above that figure. At first this contribution is a contribution towards the fixed costs, but when enough items have been sold to cover these fixed costs the business is said to break even, and any further sales mean the 'contribution' is a contribution towards the profits of the business. Thus in this happy situation an item sold for £10 whose variable costs are £3 makes a contribution of £7 to profits, all other costs having already been covered by earlier sales.

# 7.5   Revision test: marketing 2

| Answers | Questions |
| --- | --- |
| | 1 What is logistics? |
| 1 It is the art of supplying consumers with the goods they require to maintain a prosperous, sophisticated lifestyle. Formerly used about armies and fleets, today it is the general public who are the beneficiaries of complex movements of goods around the world. | 2 What is the unit load concept? |
| 2 A concept which seeks to move goods in bulk as a unit load rather than in individual packages. The devices required are stillages, pallets and containers. These are moved by fork-lift trucks, straddle carriers and container cranes, to load lorries, freight trains and cellular container ships. | 3 What are the three methods of moving goods by road? |

| Answers | Questions |
|---|---|
| 3 (a) Own-account operations<br>(b) contract hire, and<br>(c) public haulier. | **4 What are the main methods of exporting?** |
| 4 (a) Through an export merchant<br>(b) through a confirming house<br>(c) by direct selling<br>(d) by an overseas agent<br>(e) by setting up a branch office abroad. | **5 What are the five methods for securing payment for exported goods?** |
| 5 (a) Cash with order<br>(b) letter of credit<br>(c) documents against payment<br>(d) documents against acceptance<br>(e) open account terms. | **6 What is SITPRO?** |
| 6 It is the Simpler Trade Procedures Board. It is the UK representative on the international committee which seeks to make international trade easier by making documentation simpler. | **7 What is its chief contribution to simpler trade?** |
| 7 It is aligned documentation, which ensures that all types of document have the same things in the same place. Thus the exporter's name is always in the same spot on Bills of Lading, invoices, insurance policies, air waybills, etc. Even when the 'document' is electronic the same spot on the screen will be reserved for the exporter's name. | **8 What are Incoterms?** |
| 8 They are 13 agreed terms for use all over the world to decide who owns goods which are in transport and who is responsible for paying the costs incurred. At some point on the journey the goods change hands, and responsibility changes to the other party. (You might like to revise the 13 codes – see page 132 of the main text) | **9 What is E-commerce?** |
| 9 It is trade which takes place using internet technology, either via an extranet (in which companies who wish to trade with one another in a secure environment hire access to internet bandwidth to trade mutually as an extranet community) or direct with the general public using the World Wide Web. | **Go over the questions again until you are sure of all the answers. Then try the exercises in 7.6 below.** |

# 7.6   More self-assessment questions

(Answers at 7.8 below)

Here are six more questions about Chapter 7 in the main text. Take a sheet of paper and do what is required in each case. Then go through the self-assessment procedure for each question and give yourself a mark out of 100. File these sheets for revision later.

1   What is multi-modal transport?
2   What is SITPRO?
3   What is a confirming house?
4   What is a letter of credit?
5   What is a CTO?
6   What is E-commerce?

## 7.7   Examination questions

1   'The Marketing Department is a super-department which exercises control over a number of sub-departments, each of which has its part to play in the total marketing effort.' Explain this statement, referring to the various departments which come under the general control of the marketing director.
2   What is meant by the term 'marketing philosophy'? Who can develop a marketing philosophy and what purpose does it serve in an organisation?
3   What factors influence the size of the market for a particular product or service?
4   A sales manager discovers from a trade journal that the market for his particular product increased by 30 per cent in the year just ended. By consulting his sales records he finds that the sales of his firm's product actually fell by 10 per cent. What influences might have been at work to produce such a result in such a market? What policies might be pursued to remedy the situation?
5   You have been asked to prepare a sales forecast for your firm. What methods would you use?
6   What is meant by 'desk research' into a market? What sources of information for desk research are available?
7   Assess the importance to an organisation of appraising changes in the market.
8   What media outlets are likely to be of the greatest use to the following companies:
    a a manufacturer of office furniture
    b a manufacturer of household appliances
    c an importer of toys?
9   What are the advantages and disadvantages of direct mail-shots to a firm selling office equipment?
10 Discuss the methods of product pricing which might be used in a business.
11 What is meant by 'merchandising' problems in physical distribution? Illustrate your answer by several different types of merchandise and the problems which might need to be resolved.
12 The movement of goods on a world-wide scale has undergone a container revolution in the years since 1965. What are its advantages? Are there any disadvantages?
13 'Transport bridges the geographical gaps between producers and consumers.' Explain why these 'gaps' arise and illustrate your answer by examples drawn from both home and overseas trade.

14 a What is 'intermodal transport'?

b Why is it so common a feature of modern distribution?

c How is it documented and controlled?

# 7.8 Answers to self-assessment questions

(See 7.6 above)

1 Multi-modal transport is transport which uses all the modes of transport road, rail, sea and air in the best possible way. The modes of transport represent interfaces where it is possible to make the switch from one mode to another. A port is an interface between road and rail haulage on the one hand and sea transport on the other. Similarly an airport is an interface between road and rail and air transport. A railway terminal, or a junction, or a simple railway station is an interface between road and rail.

The essential feature of multi-modal transport is that the switch from one mode to the next must be quick and this means containerisation for most trades, but in some trades more packaging is enough – for example packaged timber. Transport is only helpful if it is on the move. Container cranes, straddle carriers and fork lift trucks can empty a container ship in 12 hours and send it on its way again fully loaded with a new cargo.

2 SITPRO is the Simpler Trade Procedures Board, which is the UK representative on international negotiations dealing with foreign trade. It publishes a host of useful documents, checklists and so on which are invaluable to export staff. Similar bodies exist in all trading nations.

3 A confirming house is a business house which serves foreign importers by obtaining goods they require for them. It confirms the order by adding its own name to the order, thus guaranteeing payment, so that the exporter is really dealing with a home order, and the exporting expertise is provided by the confirming house.

4 A letter of credit is a letter from a bank to an exporter advising him/her that funds are available to meet the full cost of the supply of the goods stated in the letter, provided the detailed requirements about quantity, quality, insurance, date of dispatch, documentation and so on are met. The credit will be released in settlement when a satisfactory set of documents evidencing shipment is provided to the bank under whose authority the letter of credit is issued.

5 A CTO is a combined transport operator, who arranges multi-modal movements of goods in the export trade, taking full responsibility for delivery in good order and condition at the destination address. Compensation for loss, damage or delay will be paid by the CTO who will then recover the sums paid from the carrier or other person at fault on the stage of the journey where the loss, damage or delay occurred.

6 E-commerce is trade carried on electronically, either between a group of like-minded companies who wish to trade with one another, or with the general public. In both cases it is necessary to use internet services. In the first case the community of companies who wish to trade with one another ask an ISP (internet service provider) to make a private

internet facility available to them as a group, known as an extranet, so that they can trade securely without interference from casual Internet surfers. In the second case those who wish to trade with the general public may do so, but they are well-advised to ensure secure trading either with SET (secure electronic trading) credit cards, or with a secure merchant server. Secure merchant servers are set up by the ISP to give secure arrangements when credit card details are being sent over the Internet.

# 7.9   Study tips: suggested answer to examination question 14

(See 7.7 above)

a  First we need a description of intermodal transport. Something like:
Intermodal transport is the carriage of goods from the point of origin to the point of ultimate destination by whatever mode of transport is necessary, without re-handling or re-packing. To do this we need to make up unit loads – either stuffed into containers or airborne unit load devices, or packaged (timber) or palletised. The unit load device is then transferred from one mode of transport to another, e.g. road–rail–ship–road or road–air–road, in a single movement at the interface between different modes of transport.
b  It is a common feature of modern transport because
  i    it leads to lower unit costs
  ii   it is safe – both theft and pilfering are reduced
  iii  consequently insurance charges are reduced
  iv   it is a capital-intensive system which can only be made to pay if most traffic moves that way. Consequently full loads travel by container and small loads are handled by freight forwarders with groupage depots who consolidate small loads with other compatible small loads to make up full container loads.
c  It is documented by a 'combined transport document' devised by the International Chamber of Commerce and carried under the ICC Rules for a Combined Transport Document. The essential thing here is that the CTO (combined transport operator) assumes full responsibility for the entire journey. Any complaint by consignor or consignee is settled by the CTO who then tries to identify at what point in the transit the actual loss occurred and claims from the one responsible an indemnity for the satisfaction given to the customer.

# 8　The information technology (IT) function

## 8.1　Revision test: information technology

(To consolidate your knowledge of Chapter 8 in the main text)

| Answers | Questions |
|---|---|
| | 1 What is information technology? |
| 1 It is a general term to describe a range of technologies concerned with the availability of information and its transmission around the business and scientific communities to establish a knowledge-based society. | 2 What is a database? |
| 2 The general term database is used for any collection of information which is available for reference, either in-house or (on payment of a fee) from some research foundation or trade association. | 3 What is a modem? |
| 3 A modulator-demodulator device which can turn analogue (wave) messages into digital (pulsed bitstream) messages, and vice versa. | 4 What is a computer? |
| 4 It is a device which is capable of processing data according to a program of instructions which has been fed into it and can then either put out the results in readable form or store them in a memory in machine-readable form as a database which is accessible at any time. | 5 What are the essential elements in computing? |
| 5 (a) The input of data in machine-readable form<br>(b) the processing of data according to the instruction program<br>(c) the output of the results either for immediate use or to a memory store. | 6 List the common input devices. |
| 6 (a) Punched cards<br>(b) paper tape<br>(c) keyboards or terminals<br>(d) magnetic tape<br>(e) magnetic disc<br>(f) floppy discs<br>(g) bar codes<br>(h) tags<br>(i) MICR (magnetic ink character recognition)<br>(j) OMR (optical mark recognition)<br>(k) OCR (optical character recognition). | 7 List the common output devices. |

| Answers | Questions |
| --- | --- |
| 7 (a) A VDU (visual display unit)<br>(b) line printers<br>(c) matrix printers<br>(d) daisywheel printers<br>(e) thermal printers<br>(f) ink-jet printers<br>(g) laser printers<br>(h) graph plotters<br>(i) COM (computer output to microfilm or microfiche). | **8 How fast does a computer work?** |
| 8 Speeds are reckoned in nanoseconds (ns). One nanosecond is $10^9$ seconds or 1 billionth of a second. | **9 What is meant by 'digital' transmission?** |
| 9 Instead of sending waves along a cable, for example, waves generated by the human voice, we measure the wave and send the measurements. The measurements do not deteriorate over long distances and the wave can be reconstituted at the far end. | **10 What is a LAN?** |
| 10 A local area network. This is a network of terminals and other devices, such as printers, on-line to a host computer which contains all the information of interest to terminal users. With a LAN the network is private to the company or firm concerned. | **11 What is a VAN?** |
| 11 It is a value added network in which a community of firms or companies grant access to their LANs so that they can reach into one another's computers using EDI (electronic data interchange) or DTI (direct trade input). They can enter documents, amend documents, leave messages, place orders, arrange payments and so on, in a secure way. | **12 How does the Internet improve on a VAN?** |
| 12 It gives world-wide coverage, enabling anyone in the world to contact anyone else in the world, which would be impossibly expensive for a LAN or a VAN. | **13 What is an intranet?** |
| 13 It is a private network based on internet technology whereby an ISP (Internet service provider) makes access to the net possible so that a single company can contact all its branches and outlets everywhere without fear of access by casual net surfers. | **14 What is an extranet?** |
| 14 It is like a VAN, but on a world-wide scale. The ISP makes access available to a whole community of companies, who all know one another, are all reliable and creditworthy and who want to trade with one another in a secure environment. Casual net surfers cannot access the extranet, so it is safe to make payments, make binding contracts, and so on. | **15 Go over the page again until you are quite sure of all the answers. Then try the self-assessment questions below.** |

## 8.2   Self assessment questions

(Answers at 8.4 below)

Here are 11 questions about Chapter 8 in the main text. Take a sheet of paper and do what is required in each case. Then go through the self-assessment procedure for each question and give yourself a mark out of 100. File these sheets for revision later.

1   What is a payroll package? What does it do?
2   What is a mainframe computer?
3   What is a micro-computer?
4   What is meant by 'going digital'?
5   Name four 'input devices' for getting data into a computer.
6   Name four 'output devices' for getting the results of a data-processing activity out of a computer.
7   What is a LAN? How does setting up a LAN help a company?
8   What is a VAN? In what way is it an improvement on a LAN?
9   Distinguish between an intranet and an extranet.
10 What is the Internet? How does it make e-commerce possible?
11 What is the effect of a full system of information technology on the general operation of major companies?

## 8.3   A project on a website

To build a website you start with a 'home page' which tells other net surfers who you are and where you are and what your interests are. Personal pages include information on hobbies, family and friends etc. Business pages tell about products, services, a company's mission statement, etc. You might start if you have access to a computer by saving one or two HTML codes of pages you like onto your hard disk and making a detailed study of them. You could start with http://www.instem.co.uk which is the website of the Institute of Commercial Management.

Your project is to design a personal website. If you are in business yourself it can of course be about your business. This is not a specialist book but there are many of them about. A good introductory book is *HTML in easy steps* published by Computer Step. It is widely available. Their website is http://www.computerstep.com (http stands for hyper-text mark-up language).

## 8.4   Answers to self-assessment questions

(See 8.2 above)

1  A payroll package is a set of software which computerises the activities formerly carried out by a wages clerk. The problems to be overcome will be along the following lines.

a The existing state of each employee's records must be known from the previous records kept in the wages department. They must be fed into the computer, names, addresses, PAYE codes, and so on, and stored either in the backing store disc or on a floppy disc which can be fed in each week.

b The program for manipulating the data must be input.

c The current week's information, hours worked, rate of pay, overtime, and so on, must be input.

d The computer will then work out the pay due, and update the long-term records ready for use in the following week.

e The necessary slips for the wage packets will then be printed and the details and authority for the bank to transfer funds to the employees' accounts will be sent to the BACS terminal.

2  A mainframe computer is the original type of computer set up in the 1950s and 1960s with huge capacity and serving very large companies. They offered a wide area network (WAN), with terminals all over the world being able to access the same mainframe and obtain the same data. Generally speaking they used 'bespoke software' specially written for them by teams of programmers.

3  A micro-computer is a computer which uses VLSI components (very large-scale integration). The circuits are produced in solid state form (drawn onto a chip of silicon with circuits insulated from one another). With a whole computer on a single chip these computers can be very powerful even though they are of small size.

4  'Going digital' means we convert from sending messages in wave form (because over long distances the wave tends to lose strength and background noise distorts the message sent). Instead we measure the wave 8000 times a second and instead of transmitting the wave itself we send the measurements of the wave. The wave is then reconstituted at the receiving end.

5  Four input devices: a keyboard, magnetic tape, a floppy disc, a bar code.

6  Four output devices: a VDU, a line printer, a laser printer, computer output to microfilm.

7  A LAN is a local area network. It consists of a number of terminals, printers and other devices surrounding a central host computer and on-line to it. In theory everyone in the company has access to the computer and can interrogate it on any matter that arises, from a simple database, like the in-house telephone directory, to detailed enquiries on behalf of a customer about a progress report on his/her order. A LAN makes all who have access to it feel they are as knowledgeable as everyone else, and encourages initiative and responsibility. Some companies put the salaries of all ranks on the LAN to emphasise the degree of democracy that exists in their organisation.

8  A VAN is an extension of a LAN to become part of a business 'electronic community'. The name stands for value added network. It means that the LANs of all the companies in the community can be accessed for the purpose of mutual trading in goods, services and logistical facilities. The rather limited use of a LAN internally in the company is extended to include the whole community. A particular virtue of a VAN is that all the members of the community know one another, have proven creditworthiness; their work has known quality and their trading arrangements are secure.

9  An intranet is a network of links within an international company which uses internet technology by arrangement with an ISP (an Internet service provider). It is like a LAN, but international to reach world-wide branches and subsidiaries to disseminate information, sales support, training, and so on. It is purely private to the company and its use of the Internet is walled off from casual net surfers (though it is possible to have access to the Internet for browsing purposes for the company itself).

   By contrast an extranet is a whole community of companies using internet technology for world-wide coverage but again walled off from the general Internet family. Members of the community can trade with one another, arrange logistical services, and so on, in a secure trading environment where creditworthiness and agreed terms of trade apply.

10 The Internet is a world-wide meeting place for the whole electronic community where the widest activities of information exchange, business to business dealings, academic knowledge exchange, social and hobby activities and entertainment can take place. The World Wide Web enables anyone who can afford the relatively cheap costs, to establish a web site like a magazine, where pages can be turned, information can be downloaded, e-commerce can be arranged, and so on.

   The only real defect of the Internet as far as e-commerce is concerned is that it is not of itself a secure system for payments. This is being overcome in a number of ways, for instance, by the use of SET credit cards (secure electronic transactions) and by SMSs (secure merchant servers, set up by some of the Internet service providers). These SMSs take over the payment transactions at the point where an e-commerce bargain is about to be struck, and remove the actual arrangements off the general Internet into a secure channel where outsiders cannot follow the arrangements being made.

11 The effects of a full system of information technology are:

   a Information is available to anyone with a terminal about the entire affairs of a company except that very sensitive matters may be locked off behind passwords or codes.

   b Enormous amounts of time are saved because almost anyone can call up details on the screen to amend documents, authorise work to proceed, enter movements at customs, and so on.

   c Middle layers of management are much reduced and knowledge lies with the person using the terminal at any given moment.

   d The whole system is more democratic: everyone can access everyone else and can take responsible action within the normal limits of business prudence.

   e All operations tend to be more cost effective than in traditional companies.

   f Students who have worked in such environments should add two or three further aspects from their personal experience of these matters.

## 8.5　Examination questions

1　What is information technology? What part does the telephone system play in information technology?
2　What is meant by an 'on-line' system in computing? Illustrate your answer with a description of any on-line system about which you are knowledgeable.
3　a Distinguish between hardware and software in computing.
　　b Name five input devices and five output devices.
4　What is a modem? Why are modems necessary in information technology?
5　Europe-Wide (Cambridge) PLC has taken over Growing Pains Ltd and tells the new workforce that it will soon be merged with the larger organisation by becoming part of its LAN. It appeals to all staff to attend courses to be set up in the near future to learn how to use the LAN. Explain what a LAN is and how it can affect staff favourably and unfavourably.
6　What is EDI? What is DTI? How do these techniques simplify the work of exporters?
7　Explain the terms 'Internet', 'World Wide Web', 'Internet service provider' and 'web browser'.
8　Distinguish between an intranet and an extranet.
9　What is e-commerce? How is it conducted? How may it be rendered secure for trading purposes?
10　What is C-Cure? How can it assist a company seeking to trade on the Internet?

## 8.6　Study tips: guide to the answer to question 6

EDI stands for electronic data interchange. It is the interchange, in electronic form, of information, formerly provided on documents, between interested parties. Instead of exporters, importers, forwarding agents, carriers, customs officers, and so on, relying on paper documents, they can all call up the information about a consignment on their computer screens and follow the progress of an order from start to finish. They can do this more quickly, more accurately, and in seconds, over a system designed by experts, with in-built safeguards, not subject to the errors of many individuals.

DTI stands for direct trader input. Under the EDI system anyone who has an interest in the documentation of a particular order, or cargo, can call that documentation up in its electronic form and not only see what the situation is but can directly put in any further details. For example, HM Customs can signal in less than a second that a particular cargo has been cleared for export, or for import, as the case may be, so that freight forwarders can send exports on their way, or collect imports for onward delivery to destination.

To take part in this system it is essential for all parties to use standard formats and the world format is UN EDIFACT. The SITPRO office (Simpler Trade Procedures Office) is prepared to supply information on electronic documentation. In areas where there is a VAN (a value added network) of firms using EDI, all the community of firms using the system are linked. Today, via the Internet, the traders of the whole world can be linked in such an electronic community (called an extranet) to form a private network on an international scale using Internet technology but secure from the ordinary Internet browser, who has no interest in such transactions.

# 9 Personnel department

## 9.1 Revision test: personnel

(To consolidate your knowledge of Chapter 9 in the main text)

| Answers | Questions |
|---|---|
| | **1 What is the main function of the personnel officer?** |
| 1 To secure for the organisation such staff with such skills and experience as may from time to time seem necessary, so that the firm is never starved of the human resources it needs to carry on its activities. | **2 What are the chief aspects of his/her activities?** |
| 2 (a) To recruit staff<br>(b) to induct them so that they are adequately informed of their duties and rights, and are aware of health and safety aspects<br>(c) to keep records on all employees<br>(d) to ensure compliance with all legal requirements on employment, health and safety at work, payment of wages, and so on<br>(e) to secure harmonious labour relations, and deal with difficulties that arise<br>(f) to deal with redundancy problems, warnings and dismissals, and various types of welfare arrangements. | **3 What is a personnel policy?** |
| 3 It is a body of rules approved by top management which guides the personnel officer in his/her activities. It usually covers such matters as remuneration, security of employment, promotion policy, freedom from discrimination, fair treatment, trade union policy, and so on. | **4 What is human resource planning?** |
| 4 It is a conscious process of reviewing personnel needs for the conceivable future to see what types and qualities of staff will be needed and taking steps to train or recruit staff with the required skills. | **5 Why is documentation important in personnel work?** |
| 5 Because we need sound records on all our employees, to prove that we have always acted within the law in recruitment, induction, disciplinary procedures, dismissal, and so on. We need to be able to show absence of racial or sexual discrimination. We also need to be able to give references after staff have left our employ. | **6 What is the use of job descriptions?** |

| Answers | Questions |
|---|---|
| 6 (a) They force the manager requiring staff to think about the job and its various activities so that he/she has a clear picture of the duties to be performed.<br>(b) This helps build a picture of the person required, the skills, qualifications and so on needed.<br>(c) The job description helps in deciding comparability with other jobs, the scale of pay, and so on. | **7 Why do we often recruit staff from the friends and relatives of present staff?** |
| 7 (a) Because it is cheap (there are no advertising costs)<br>(b) because the applicants are keen to give satisfaction so that they do not let the relative down<br>(c) it raises staff morale to some extent (the danger is they may be all of the same ethnic group and infringe the Race Relations Act). | **8 What is induction?** |
| 8 It is the process of introducing new employees to the firm, to welcome them, tell them of the employer's rules, warn them of hazards, tell them about disciplinary procedures and introduce them to their supervisors and colleagues. | **9 Why is training important?** |
| 9 (a) To start the employee off in his/her job performance<br>(b) to broaden his/her experience as the months pass<br>(c) to develop staff of the right calibre by a 'grow your own' policy for building teams of people for promotion<br>(d) to provide eventually fully professionally qualified staff who know everything they need to know to run the firm/company. | **10 What is performance appraisal?** |
| 10 It is a procedure for reviewing on a regular basis the level of performance achieved by staff in both ordinary working circumstances and in the pursuit of long-term training. It greatly assists human resource planning and raises staff morale by requiring management to take an interest in staff and not overlook their efforts, however humdrum the level. It may be linked to merit awards and pay increases. | **11 What are the requirements about termination of employment and dismissal?** |
| 11 Unfair dismissal can be the cause of an action before an industrial tribunal. All employers should have written rules and disciplinary proceedings which are made available to employees to show them what types of conduct are considered unsatisfactory and how such misconduct will be dealt with. | **12 What is labour turnover?** |
| 12 It is the rapidity with which staff leave, on average. Usually stated as a percentage calculated on the formula:<br>Labour turnover = $\dfrac{\text{No. of leavers in the period} \times 100}{\text{Average no. of employees in the period}}$ | **13 What are the disadvantages of high labour turnover?** |
| 13 (a) Heavy recruitment costs<br>(b) heavy training costs<br>(c) spoilt work<br>(d) increased chance of accidents<br>(e) low staff morale and general uncertainty. | **14 Go over the questions again until you are sure of all the answers. Then try the self-assessment questions overleaf.** |

## 9.2   Self-assessment questions

(Answers at 9.4 below)

Here are eight questions about Chapter 9 in the main text. Take a sheet of paper and do what is required in each case. Then go through the self-assessment procedure for each question and give yourself a mark out of 100. File these sheets for revision later.

1  What is the chief function of the personnel officer?
2  What are the alternative attitudes to promotion policy?
3  What are the stages in a review of human resources?
4  What is 'discrimination' in terms of employment policy?
5  What is an employee data folder?
6  What is a personnel requisition form?
7  What is an interview record? Why is it important?
8  State the case for becoming a full, professionally qualified member of staff in your own discipline (field of endeavour).

## 9.3   An assignment on personnel matters

Draw up a detailed job description for any post you care to envisage, either in your own industry or profession, or in an occupation which interests you. From this job description then deduce the characteristics you would look for in applicants, the field of background education and experience they should have, and so on. Then write an advertisement to be published in a trade or professional paper, making it as attractive as you can. Present your assignment in three parts:

1  the job description
2  guidance notes to the interviewing panel about the type of person required, and
3  the advertisement.

## 9.4   Answers to self-assessment questions

1  The chief function of the personnel officer is to secure for the firm or the company human resources in such numbers and of such qualities as may be required from time to time, either by recruitment from outside or by a 'grow your own' process inside the organisation through systematic training and development programmes.
2  The alternative attitudes to promotion policy are promotion from within the organisation wherever possible and open recruitment from both within and from outside. The former encourages company loyalty and raises staff morale; the latter ensures that new blood is infused into the organisation so that it does not become too inbred. The latter

method is more likely to lead to an ethnic and sexual balance within the firm in compliance with the Race Relations Act and the equal opportunities legislation.

3 The stages in a review of human resources are:

a to review the existing situation

b to assess the future situation

c to draw up a plan of the future organisation

d to make detailed plans for training staff

e if necessary recruit from outside any specialist staff where the shortage cannot be relieved by training existing staff.

4 Discrimination is a term used in the Race Relations Act 1976 and the Sex Discrimination Act 1975 (as amended). It refers to a tendency to treat certain groups less favourably than other groups. For example, if an employer does not offer a post to a person on racial grounds or because the applicant is a woman, that is discrimination. Similarly, to offer a person the post at a lesser rate of pay for these reasons would be discrimination. The responsibility for ensuring that equal opportunities are provided rests with employers.

5 An employee data folder is a stationery device which records the basic details about an employee and acts as a receptacle for copies of all forms, contracts, notices, and so on, supplied to or relating to the employee. It is opened on recruitment, and retained on file during employment. It may be archived after the employee has left the employment but is retained indefinitely since it is often necessary to give references even years after the employee's resignation.

6 A personnel requisition form is a form made out by the head of a requisitioning department describing the type of post that has to be filled, the qualifications looked for in the applicant, and so on. The form is sent to the personnel officer, who will attempt to fill the post, either by transfer of a suitable existing member of staff or by advertising its availability.

7 An interview record is a form used at an interview by each member of the panel to record his/her impressions of the applicant and his/her recommendations about appointment. It is important in that it is evidence of a proper consideration of the applicant should allegations of discriminatory behaviour be alleged in any complaint to an industrial tribunal.

8 A fully professionally qualified person usually has achieved that status in two ways: by passing examinations in the background theory which is important to the profession and by practical experience in the working situation over a period of several years. This gives the best possible grounding for everyday employment in the profession at the highest level and is the sort of qualification to which all alert, energetic and ambitious persons should aspire.

# 9.5    Examination questions

1   What are the functions of a personnel department in a large company? In answering this question you should particularly refer to the likely status of the personnel officer and his/her responsibilities. Are any limitations placed upon his/her powers?

2   a What is a job description?

    b What useful purposes do job descriptions serve in the administration of large businesses?

3   As deputy to the personnel manager, you have been asked to advertise forthcoming vacancies for two members of staff. How would you undertake this task?

4   What are the specific responsibilities of the personnel department in a large firm?

5   Why is human resource planning important? What problems may arise in drafting a human resource plan for an organisation?

6   What factors do you consider enhance staff morale?

7   You have been asked by your manager to draw up a pre-interview check-list for the procedures to be used in handling applications for a job in your department. Write the check-list you would use to process the applications for this position and explain the importance of the items you selected.

8   'Generally speaking, a stable labour force is advantageous to any company; a high rate of labour turnover involves many hidden costs.' Discuss this statement, explaining how labour turnover may be measured and pinpointing some of the hidden costs referred to.

9   What is an induction programme? What opportunities does it give to (a) management and (b) new personnel? Draw up a list of ten items you would consider should be mentioned in such a programme.

10 It is the custom in your company to hold 'merit ratings' in October – for all junior and middle management staff – with a right of appeal should a merit award not be made. Increases in salary then start on 1 January. What matters should be considered in assessing a merit rating and what records should be kept to ensure a fair appraisal? How is it of use to management?

11 Negotiation is a task that all managers perform. What is 'negotiation' and what skills are required if negotiation is to be successful?

12 Assess the importance of industrial relations to the economic performance of industry. How may good industrial relations be fostered?

13 Write the text of an advertisement for an employment opportunity in any firm with which you are familiar. Give a description of the job concerned, the salary payable, the qualifications required and the deadline for applications. Invite applicants to write to you, as personnel officer of the firm concerned.

14 'Prosperity increases labour turnover, and so does uncertainty.' What is 'labour turnover'; what effect does it have on an enterprise and how may we avoid it in times of prosperity, or uncertainty (for example, during a takeover bid)?

# 9.6  Study tips: a suggested answer to question 14

1  First we need a definition of labour turnover. Something like:
Labour turnover is a measure of the rapidity with which labour takes employment and then leaves to take a job elsewhere. It is usually expressed as a percentage of the labour force. This percentage is found using the formula:

$$\frac{\text{No. of leavers in the period} \times 100}{\text{Average no. of employees in the period}}$$

Thus if 77 people leave out of an average body of employees totalling 685 the percentage is:
77/685 x 100 = 11.2%

2  The effects of labour turnover are:
   a Increased recruitment costs – advertising, interviewing, and so on.
   b Increased induction and training costs – to settle new employees in and teach them the procedures and routines.
   c Spoilage and wastage during the training periods.
   d A generally unsettled atmosphere, with some sections of the business working at less than optimum level.
   e Low morale – leaving is infectious.

3  In times of prosperity when there is a shortage of skilled labour it is difficult to stop good people going elsewhere. We should try:
   a Keeping our wage payments comparable with others elsewhere.
   b Making sure fringe benefits are available to key staff so that moving costs them more than just loss of wages – they lose benefits not available elsewhere.
   c Closely investigating motives for leaving of each leaver. Is there some mismanagement occurring?

4  In times of uncertainty we should try to reduce labour turnover by:
   a Reassuring those whose employment is secure despite the changes.
   b Clearly explaining the needs for the changes and the future prospects if the changes are implemented.

# 10 The accounting function

## 10.1 Revision test: the accounting function

(To consolidate your knowledge of Chapter 10 in the main text)

| Answers | Questions |
|---|---|
| | **1 What is the basic system of accounting?** |
| 1 Double-entry book-keeping. | **2 What are the basic elements of a double-entry system?** |
| 2 (a) Every transaction starts with the issue of an original document<br>(b) the documents are recorded in a book of original entry, such as the Cash Book, Purchases Day Book, Sales Day Book, and so on (or, of course, these may be computerised in some way)<br>(c) the entries are then posted to the ledger, the chief book of account, each page of which is called an account<br>(d) at suitable intervals we take out a Trial Balance of the ledger<br>(e) from this Trial Balance we draw up a Trading Account and a Profit and Loss Account to find the profits of the business<br>(f) the residue of the Trial Balance then gives us a Balance Sheet, which is a list of the assets and liabilities at a given moment in time, the last second of the last day of the financial year. | **3 What are the functions of the accountant?** |
| 3 (a) To raise money to provide the original capital<br>(b) to advise on financial decisions on resource allocation<br>(c) to carry out the routine accounting activities<br>(d) to exercise budgetary control, and other financial controls<br>(e) to carry out internal audit procedures<br>(f) to prepare the final accounts and report to management about profitability<br>(g) to alert management early on all matters which appear likely to cause problems or to interfere with the attainment of the company's objectives. | **4 What is fixed capital?** |

| Answers | Questions |
|---|---|
| 4 Capital tied up in fixed assets, which last a long time and give enduring services to the company (for example, land and buildings, plant and machinery, office equipment, motor vehicles, furniture and fittings). | **5 What is working capital?** |
| 5 Capital tied up in current assets which only last a short time, such as stock, consumable materials, debtors and liquid assets (money – cash in hand or cash at the bank). | **6 What is management by exceptions?** |
| 6 It is the system whereby financial and other records are subject to regular appraisals by the submission of 'returns' from branches, or by computerised controls, which draw attention to exceptional developments. Figures within the permitted limits are not investigated, but anything outside the ordinary run of events is rigorously investigated. | **7 What are standard costs?** |
| 7 Carefully assembled cost figures which take account of raw materials, components and labour used in good average conditions. They are then compared with actual costs, and any variance calls for investigation. | **8 Supposing a variance is caused by outside forces which we cannot control?** |
| 8 We can only pass the increased cost on to the customer in our price. | **9 Supposing we can control the variance?** |
| 9 We discover the cause and put it right. This may mean closer supervision, better training, dismissal of staff if theft is involved, and so on. | **10 What is an internal audit procedure?** |
| 10 It is a procedure introduced by the accountant to check any aspect of the business where money, stock or valuable assets are handled to ensure that correct procedures are being followed in a climate of honest business activity. | **11 What is an Appropriation Account?** |
| 11 One in which the profits of a business are appropriated to particular uses, either giving them away to the partners or shareholders or putting them into reserves to expand the business. | **12 If profit is put into reserve, what happens to the actual money made?** |
| 12 It is available to buy fixed assets, or current assets (stock) or to finance debtors during a credit period. In other words it enables the business to grow. | **13 Go over the questions again until you are sure of all the answers. Then try the self-assessment questions below.** |

# 10.2 Self-assessment questions

Here are eight questions about Chapter 10 in the main text. Take a sheet of paper and answer the questions. Then go through the self-assessment procedure for each question and give yourself a mark out of 100. File these sheets for revision later.

1  What is accounting?
2  What is double-entry book-keeping?

3  What are the rules for double-entry book-keeping?
4  What is overtrading?
5  What is undertrading?
6  How do businesses usually grow?
7  What is a cash flow budget?
8  What is an internal audit?

# 10.3  A project on simple accounts

Fig 10.1 of the main text is a chart showing how double-entry book-keeping works. Your project is to do the following things:

a  Collect examples of each of the documents referred to, in so far as you can. People do not like giving up documents, but you should be able to collect some from your own purchases, or family transactions. You want:

i    A top copy of an invoice (for something you purchased).

ii   More difficult – the second copy of an invoice – for something you sold.

iii  A top copy of a credit note (for something you returned; a 'purchases returned' credit note.

iv   Again, more difficult – the second copy of a credit note (for something returned to you from a customer); a sales returned credit note.

v    A cheque received from someone – photocopy it before you pay it in.

vi   A cheque paid to someone – photocopy it before you send it off to them.

vii  A petty cash voucher for something you purchased. This could be a till receipt.

viii A more durable document (like an HP agreement, or a loan agreement, or a mortgage. Photocopy it for your collection.

b  Write short notes (five to eight lines) to explain the double entry on four documents.

i    The top copy of an invoice for one of your purchases was £500 for goods for resale (two bicycles actually). You bought them from Reliable Bicycles Ltd and will pay within 30 days. Which account would you debit and which would you credit?

ii   The cheque for £475 sent to Reliable Cycles later in the month (£500 less 5% settlement discount). Which account would you debit and which would you credit? You have to make the entries clear the £500 debt to Reliable Cycles!

iii  A petty cash voucher for the purchase of petrol £19.80 in cash.

iv   A loan document you hold is for a loan from your bank of £500, to be placed in your current account. It also mentions a charge for arranging the loan (£20), the total being repayable in 12 monthly installments. Which accounts would you make an entry in, and on which side.

The answers to these questions are given in Section 10.7 below.

# 10.4 Answers to self-assessment questions

1 Accounting is the art of controlling a business by keeping accurate routine records from which the profitability and general state of the business may be discovered, and instituting a variety of controls over expenditure and receipts, so that expenditures outside budget are discovered and corrected and the business is never starved of cash resources because of bad debts.

2 Double-entry book-keeping is the basis of all accounting records. Every transaction results in a double entry, one (or more) accounts receiving value and another (or others) giving value.

3 The rules for double entries in accounting are 'Debit the account that receives goods, or services, or money and credit the account that gives goods, or services, or money.'

4 Overtrading is where a firm or company expands its manufacturing or trading capacity beyond the point where it can adequately finance the day-to-day activities. Expansion requires larger wage bills, larger stocks, an increased number of debtors (often with longer credit periods) and the result is a shortage of funds for working capital. This requires the firm or company to borrow money and profits are creamed off to banks and other lenders.

5 Undertrading is where a business has surplus funds available and could, if it wished, expand the business to use these funds profitably.

6 Businesses usually grow by ploughing back profits to expand activities by buying more plant and machinery, motor vehicles and so on. The profits thus used are no longer available as dividends for shareholders or as profits for the owners, but instead represent an increase in the value of the business. The extra funds are re-invested in extra capital assets which enlarge the business.

7 A cash flow budget is a budget which envisages future receipts and expenditures so as to reveal any possible surplus or deficit in the months ahead. Thus it is possible to anticipate an adverse situation and arrange overdrafts or loans as required, while a surplus in prospect may indicate a suitable moment to purchase a new machine, motor vehicle, and so on.

8 An internal audit is an investigation to examine the records of a department where cash, consumables and other assets are concerned to detect improper use of funds or other resources.

# 10.5 Examination questions

*(Note: Numerical answers are provided at the end of this chapter.)*

1 What is a Trial Balance? What is a Trading and Profit and Loss Account? What is the link between them?

2 Explain the term 'cash flows' and show why it is important for the successful operation of a business.

3  R. Martin's cash flow estimates for the month ahead are as follows: cash in hand on 1 October 20.... £625; cash at the bank £8080; cash sales for the month £4425; credit sales for the month £5865; credit sales in September were £6426 and half are expected to pay in October; sales prior to September and still outstanding for payment total £5560 of which £4000 is confidently expected in October. Cash purchases are expected to be £4660 in October and it is also proposed to pay £3580 for goods received in August and September. Wages are expected to be £8250 in the month, and other overheads £1080. A capital item (a new vehicle) is expected in October and one quarter of the price of £18 500 will be paid on delivery. The proprietor will take drawings of £600 in the month.

   a Work out a cash flow statement for the month of October and the anticipated bank balance at the end of the month assuming cash in hand at that time will be restricted to £200.

   b What would you advise Martin to do in view of this budget, before the month begins?

4  Newmark Ltd has an authorised capital of £400 000 divided into 400 000 ordinary shares of £1 each. The following balances were extracted from the books at 31 December 20...:

|  | £ |
|---|---|
| Ordinary capital (fully paid) | 320 000 |
| General reserve (1 January 20...) | 15 000 |
| Profit and Loss Account (credit balance 1 January 20... | 2 590 |
| Profit for year to 31 December 20... | 79 620 |
| Fixtures and fittings at cost | 16 000 |
| Machinery at cost | 155 000 |
| Provisions for depreciation: | |
| Fixtures and fittings | 8 600 |
| Machinery | 50 000 |
| Freehold premises at cost | 168 000 |
| Stock | 32 500 |
| Sundry debtors | 7 130 |
| Sundry creditors | 9 440 |
| Bank balance | 108 620 |
| Debenture (Helpful Bank PLC) | 2 000 |

The directors have decided to transfer £15 000 to reserve and to recommend a dividend of 10 percent on the issued ordinary shares. They also decide to put £25 000 in corporation tax reserve.

Prepare the Appropriation Account of the company for the year ended December 20.... and a Balance Sheet as at that date, in vertical style.

5 Polarised Lighting Ltd has an authorised capital of £300 000 divided into 300 000 ordinary shares of £1 each. The following balances were extracted from the books at 31 December 20....:

| | £ |
|---|---|
| Ordinary capital issued (fully paid) | 150 000 |
| General reserve (1 January 20…) | 25 000 |
| Profit and Loss Appropriation Account (credit balance 1 January 20....) | 12 725 |
| 7% Debentures | 40 000 |
| Profit for year to 31 December 20… | 76 255 |
| Fixtures and fittings at cost | 23 520 |
| Plant and machinery at cost | 48 500 |
| Provisions for depreciation: | |
|    Fixtures and fittings | 2 520 |
|    Machinery | 6 500 |
| Freehold premises at cost | 112 000 |
| Stock | 37 250 |
| Cash in hand | 380 |
| Sundry debtors | 5 250 |
| Stock of advertising material | 4 350 |
| Sundry creditors | 3 250 |
| Bank balance | 85 000 |

The directors have decided to transfer £25 000 to general reserve and £30 000 to reserve for corporation tax.
They recommend a dividend of 15 percent on the issued ordinary shares.

Prepare the Appropriation Account for the company for the year ended December 20… and a Balance Sheet as at that date, in vertical style.

# 10.6  Study tips: answer to question 5

*Appropriation Account of Polarised Lighting Ltd for year ending 31 December 20....*

| 20... | | £ | 20... | | £ |
|---|---|---|---|---|---|
| Dec. 31 | Reserve for corporation tax | 30 000 | Jan 1 | Balance | 12 725 |
| | General reserve | 25 000 | Dec 31 | Profit for year | 76 255 |
| | Ordinary dividend | 22 500 | | | 88 980 |
| | Balance | 11 480 | | | |
| | | £88 980 | | | £88 980 |

| | | | 20... | | £ |
|---|---|---|---|---|---|
| | | | Jan 1 | Balance | 11 480 |

*Balance Sheet as at 31 December 20…*

| Fixed Assets | At cost | Depreciation to date | Value |
|---|---|---|---|
| Land and buildings | 112 000 | – | 112 000 |
| Plant and machinery | 48 500 | 6 500 | 42 000 |
| Fixtures and fittings | 23 520 | 2 520 | 21 000 |
| | 184 020 | 9 020 | 175 000 |

| Current Assets | £ |
|---|---|
| Stock | 37 250 |
| Stock of advertising material | 4 350 |
| Debtors | 5 250 |
| Cash at bank | 85 000 |
| Cash in hand | 380 |
| | 132 230 |

| *less* Current Liabilities: | | |
|---|---|---|
| Creditors | 3 250 | |
| Ordinary dividend | 22 500 | |
| | | 25 750 |
| | | 106 480 |
| Net Assets | | £281 480 |

**Financed by:**

| *Ordinary shareholders' interest in the company* | | *Authorised* | *Issued* |
|---|---|---|---|
| Ordinary shares of £1 fully paid | | 300 000 | 150 000 |

| *Revenue reserves* | | |
|---|---|---|
| General reserve | 25 000 | |
| + Additions | 25 000 | |
| | 50 000 | |
| Balance on Appropriation A/c | 11 480 | |
| | | 61 480 |
| **Ordinary shareholders' equity** | | 211 480 |
| 7% Debentures | | 40 000 |
| Reserve for corporation tax | | 30 000 |
| | | £281 480 |

# 10.7 Answers to numerical questions above

3 R. Martin has an overdraft of £2652, and should make overdraft arrangements accordingly.
4 Newmark Ltd, balance on Appropriation Account £10 210; net assets total £387 210; ordinary shareholders' interest in the company £360 210.
5 See fully worked answer on page 66.

# 10.8 Answers to project questions above

(See 10.3 above)

i    Debit Purchase A/C £500.00 Credit Reliable BicyclesLtd £500
     (They are now a creditor, to whom we owe money)
ii   Reliable Cycles are debited with £500.00 to extinguish our debt.
     Credit Bank A/C £475.00 and Credit Discount Received Account £25.00
     (This is a bit of extra profit – a reward for paying promptly).
iii  Debit Motor Expenses A/C £19.80, credit Petty Cash A/C £19.80
iv   Debit Bank A/C with £500.00 Debit Bank charges A/C £20.00
     Credit Bank Loan A/C £520.00 (The Bank is a creditor for the full amount we owe).
     There will also be an interest charge later.

# 11 Office administration

## 11.1 Revision test: office administration

(To consolidate your knowledge of Chapter 10 in the main text)

| Answers | Questions |
| --- | --- |
| | 1 What is the role of the general administration officer? |
| 1 It is a 'sweeper-up' role, taking charge of all administrative activities that do not lie within the clear functional responsibilities of specialist directors such as the marketing director, the accountant, and so on. | 2 What are some of the chief areas of responsibility? |
| 2 Supervision of premises, equipment, furniture, caretaking, cleaning, the working environment, health and safety at work, clerical and secretarial services, reprographics, telephone and intercom facilities, computerised systems and security. | 3 How are these duties generally described in modern professional circles? |
| 3 As 'facilities management'. | 4 What are the chief points about office location? |
| 4 (a) Preferably as central as possible <br> (b) at reasonable rent (perhaps with official aid on relocation) <br> (c) close to good rail, motorway, airport or ferry facilities <br> (d) where staff will have a good quality of life. | 5 What are the chief types of offices? |
| 5 (a) Open plan <br> (b) cubicle offices. | 6 What are the advantages of open-plan offices? |
| 6 (a) Cheap to construct <br> (b) democratic <br> (c) simple layouts, aesthetically attractive and adaptable to changing circumstances <br> (d) easy communication between staff. | 7 What are the chief clerical duties? |
| 7 (a) Routine procedures, such as mail shots, supply of samples, sale of catalogues and other publications <br> (b) record-keeping, customer details, complaints <br> (c) filing and archiving <br> (d) calculations, statistical records and returns. | 8 What are the main parts of a business letter? |
| 8 (a) The names and addresses of both parties to the correspondence <br> (b) the references and the date <br> (c) the salutation | *(continues opposite)* |

| Answers | Questions |
|---|---|
| (d) the subject heading<br>(e) the opening paragraph<br>(f) the body of the letter<br>(g) the complimentary close<br>(h) the signature, and<br>(i) the enclosures and distribution. | **9 List the elements of an agenda.** |
| 9 (a) Minutes of the last meeting<br>(b) signature as a true record<br>(c) matters arising<br>(d) the detailed agenda items as agreed between the secretary and the chairperson<br>(e) any other business<br>(f) date of next meeting. Points of order may be raised at any time. | **10 What are the chief points about organising conferences or functions of any kind?** |
| 10 (a) Appoint someone, or a subcommittee, to be in charge<br>(b) think the whole thing through very carefully<br>(c) contact speakers, leading guests, and so on<br>(d) book accommodation and other necessary items<br>(e) design brochures, advertising material, badges for delegates, and so on<br>(f) dispatch invitations and deal with responses<br>(g) appoint enough staff to manage the affair properly, especially low-level staff<br>(h) have everything ready on the day, and fully staffed<br>(i) ensure plenty of help in clearing up<br>(j) attend to all follow-up activities. | **11 Define delegation.** |
| 11 Delegation is the transfer to lower-level staff of the responsibility for performing a given set of tasks or duties, and the conferring upon them of sufficient authority to enable the duties to be carried out. | **12 Go over the questions again until you are sure of all the answers. Then try the self-assessment questions below.** |

# 11.2 Self-assessment questions

(Answers at 11.4 below)

Here are eight questions about Chapter 11 in the main text. Take a sheet of paper and answer the questions. Then go through the self-assessment procedure for each question and give yourself a mark out of 100. File these sheets for revision later.

1   What are clerical activities?
2   What is meant by 'facilities management'?
3   What can be said in favour of cubicle offices?
4   What is meant by a 'routine procedure'?

5  What is meant in business correspondence by:
   a the salutation
   b the subject heading
   c the subscription
   d the distribution?

# 11.3  A practical exercise on filing alphabetically

*Practical exercise 1*
Select the correct first indexing unit in the following names (for the answers see p. 72)
a  Alfred J. Marshall
b  Peter R. Cummings
c  Daniel Daniels
d  M.V.T. Potterton and Co. Ltd
e  Liverpool Wheat Exchange
f  R.S.V. Paterson & Co. Ltd
g  Zoological Gardens of Chester
h  Chartered Institute of Transport
i  Terry Mendoza (Photographics) Ltd
j  Seamen's Society

*Practice exercise 2*
Arrange the following names in alphabetical order, correctly indexed (for the answers see p. 72).
a  Peter Jones, Daniel Wheddon, Harry Hawke
b  Silas T. Lark, Samuel P. Larkin, Ruby M. Lazarus
c  A.J. Cronin, Charles Dickens, Rudyard Kipling, H. Melville

*Practice exercise 2a*
Arrange the following names in correct sequence (for the answers see p. 72).
a  R. Chambers, R. Chalmers, Eric Chalmers, Edith Chumleigh
b  R. Fortescue & Sons Ltd, R. Fortescue, R. Forte, Peter Forth
c  Howard Proctor Ltd, Peter Howard, P.T. Howard
d  Gurr & Co. Ltd, Ben Gunn, B. Gunn Ltd, B. Gnu, B. Gnutsen
e  R. Marshall & Co. Ltd, R. Marshall, Rosemary Marshall
f  P. Lane, Penny Lane, Penelope Lane, Penelope P. Langdon
g  Glover & Sons Ltd, Grover & Co., Glouceston Ltd, P. Grimes Ltd
h  Murray, John Murray, John Martin, Joan Martindale
i  Lyons of Dumbarton, Lyons of Doncaster, Lyons of Lyonnesse
j  Armstrong (Dover) Ltd, Armstrong (Middlesex) Ltd, Armstrong (Manchester) Ltd

*Practice exercise 3*

List the following groups of names in correct alphabetical order (for the answers see p. 72).

a  Mrs M.L. Gilbert, M. Gilbert, OBE, Professor Martin Gilbert
b  Dr Howard Jones, MD, R. Jones, DFC, Mrs Rita Jones
c  Mrs D.W. Heather, Lady Doreen Heather, Sir Dennis Heather, CH

*Practice exercise 4*

List the following groups of names in correct alphabetical order (for the answers see p. 72).

a  Thomas O'Leary, Michael O'Loughlin, Peter Osgood, Mary O'Callaghan
b  Peter Du Bois, Oscar Van Tromp, Pieter de Raat, Roger McCardy
c  Thomas McEvoy, Peter MacIlven, Roger McInnes, the Right Honourable Hugh McGrath (assume that a special place is reserved for Mac and Mc).
d  Saint, A., St Andrew's School, St Aloysius College, St Trinian's, Saint James' Academy
e  Roberto da Costa, Rita de St Angelo, Irene d'Eye, Peter de Gout

*Practice exercise 5*

Arrange these groups in correct order (for the answers see p. 72).

a  Ian Forbes-Adam, Roberta Forbes-Robertson, Mildred Forbes-Poynter
b  Peter Knapp, Roger Knapp-Fisher, Alan Knapp-Anderson
c  Klockner-Knoeller Ltd, Arthur Klockner, Jane Klockner-Stubel
d  Alan Ross, Peter Ross-Whyte, Clifford Ross-Whittingham, David Ross-White
e  Ultra-electric Co. Ltd, Ultra-violet Ray Co. Ltd, Ultra-sonics Ltd

*Practice exercise 6*

Arrange these groups in correct order (for the answers see p. 73).

a  J.R. South and Co. Ltd, South Western Gas Board, Southern Railway
b  Harry South, South Hampstead Cricket Club, H.L. South
c  W.C. Stewart, Stew and Simmer, Stewart Ward Coins Ltd
d  Whiter Wash Co., White Sea Canal Co., R.J. White
e  Sweeney Todd, Todd, S.J., Today's Wear, Toddlers' Wear
f  Canvey Island Motors Ltd, J.R. Canvey, John Canvey, Peter Canvey

## Answer section

The answers to the practice exercises are given below.

**Practice exercise 1**
The first indexing units are:
a  Marshall
b  Cummings
c  Daniels
d  Potterton
e  Liverpool
f  Paterson
g  Chester
h  Transport
i  Mendoza
j  Seamen's

**Practice exercise 2**
a  Hawke, Harry
　 Jones, Peter
　 Wheddon, Daniel
b  Lark, Silas T.
　 Larkin, Samuel P.
　 Lazarus, Ruby M.
c  Cronin, A.J.
　 Dickens, Charles
　 Kipling, Rudyard
　 Melville, H.

**Practice exercise 2a**
a  Chalmers, Eric
　 Chalmers, R.
　 Chambers, R.
　 Chumleigh, Edith
b  Forte, R.
　 Fortescue, R.
　 Fortescue, R. & Sons Ltd
　 Forth, Peter
c  Howard, P.T.
　 Howard, Peter
　 Howard Proctor Ltd
d  Gnu, B.
　 Gnutsen, B.
　 Gunn, B. Ltd

Gunn, Ben
Gurr & Co. Ltd
e  Marshall, R.
　 Marshall, R. & Co. Ltd
　 Marshall, Rosemary
f  Lane, P.
　 Lane, Penelope
　 Lane, Penny
　 Langdon, Penelope P.
g  Glouceston Ltd
　 Glover & Sons Ltd
　 Grimes, P. Ltd
　 Grover & Co.
h  Martin, John
　 Martindale, Joan
　 Murray
　 Murray, John
i  Lyons, Doncaster, of
　 Lyons, Dumbarton, of
　 Lyons, Lyonnesse, of
j  Armstrong (Dover) Ltd
　 Armstrong (Manchester)
　　 Ltd
　 Armstrong (Middlesex)
　　 Ltd

**Practice exercise 3**
a  Gilbert, M., OBE
　 Gilbert, Mrs M.L.
　 Gilbert, Professor Martin
b  Jones, Dr Howard, MD
　 Jones, R., DFC
　 Jones, Mrs Rita
c  Heather, Mrs D.W.
　 Heather, Sir Dennis, CH
　 Heather, Lady Doreen

**Practice exercise 4**
a  O'Callaghan, Mary
　 O'Leary, Thomas

O'Loughlin, Michael
　 Osgood, Peter
b  De Raat, Pieter
　 Du Bois, Peter
　 McCardy, Roger
　 Van Tromp, Oscar
c  McEvoy, Thomas
　 McGrath, the Rt Hon.
　　 Hugh
　 MacIlven, Peter
　 MacInnes, Roger
d  Saint, A.
　 St Aloysius College
　 St Andrew's School
　 Saint James' Academy
　 St Trinian's
e  Da Costa, Roberto
　 De Gout, Peter
　 De St Angelo, Rita
　 D'Eye, Irene

**Practice exercise 5**
a  Forbes-Adam, Ian
　 Forbes-Poynter, Mildred
　 Forbes-Robertson,
　　 Roberta
b  Knapp, Peter
　 Knapp-Anderson, Alan
　 Knapp-Fisher, Roger
c  Klockner, Arthur
　 Klockner-Knoeller, Ltd
　 Klockner-Stubel, Jane
d  Ross, Alan
　 Ross-White, David
　 Ross-Whittingham,
　　 Clifford
　 Ross-Whyte, Peter
e  Ultra-electric Co. Ltd
　 Ultra-sonics Ltd
　 Ultra-violet Ray Co. Ltd

*Practice exercise 6*

a South J.R. and Co. Ltd
  Southern Railway
  South Western Gas
    Board
b South, H.L.
  South, Harry
  South Hampstead
    Cricket Club

c Stew and Simmer
  Stewart, W.C.
  Stewart Ward Coins Ltd
d White, R.J.
  Whiter Wash Co.
  White Sea Canal Co.
e Today's Wear
  Todd, S.J.
  Todd, Sweeney

Toddlers' Wear
f Canvey, J.R.
  Canvey, John
  Canvey, Peter
  Canvey Island Motors
    Ltd

# 11.4 Answers to self-assessment questions

1 Clerical activities are those performed by clerks: office employees with skills in writing, calculating, record-keeping, book-keeping, and so on. Although many clerical activities are routine the term does not necessarily imply low-level activities and many high officers in Parliament, or the law, or local government, are called clerks.

2 Facilities management is the latest term for business administration; it refers to the work of that type of professional administrator who has responsibility for premises, equipment, information technology and personnel in the modern, large-scale, computerised office complex.

3 Cubicle offices are private, quiet, single-purpose offices dedicated to a particular aspect of administrative activity, where important decisions can be taken undisturbed by the hurly-burly of activity associated with open-plan offices.

4 A routine procedure is one which has been devised to deal quickly and simply with a set of circumstances which are likely to be repeated many times. Thus the procedure for acknowledging, documenting and fulfiling customers' orders is repeated endlessly, as a matter of routine, in all trading enterprises. Every organisation has its routines – a violent death is an unusual event to most of us, but to the crime squad, the coroner and the undertaker it is routine.

5 a The salutation is the greeting at the start of a letter: Dear Sir, Dear Madam, or Dear Mr Smith.
  b The subject heading tells the addressee the subject of the letter, and helps to direct it to the correct department when opened in the mail inwards section.
  c The subscription is the complimentary closure at the end of the letter: Yours faithfully, Yours sincerely, and so on.
  d The distribution list appears at the end of the letter and lists any people, apart from the addressee, who are to receive a copy.

6 Word-processing software enables a secretary to produce high-quality correspondence for dispatch to addresses, but it also retains a copy in the computer's memory for later updating or amendment. The memory will also store an agreed range of paragraphs, salutations, complimentary closes, standard letters, and so on, which lighten the secretary's load considerably.

7 Delegation is the transfer to subordinates of the responsibility for performing a given task, or range of tasks, with authority to make management decisions as required, consistent with the duties to be performed.

8 a A subcommittee is a small committee, usually not more than three people, to pursue some activity or investigate some problem on behalf of the main committee from which the members have been drawn.

   b 'Through the chair' is a request made to those wishing to speak to a meeting which prevents them speaking while other people are speaking. The chair only recognises one person at a time, and speaking through the chair prevents the meeting becoming disorderly, with several people trying to speak at once.

   c 'Lie on the table' is a term used when it seems impossible for those present to reach any conclusion about an item on the agenda (perhaps because a particular person is absent or some vital information is not yet to hand). A matter left to 'lie on the table' is not closed, but will be considered further at a more appropriate moment.

## 11.5 Examination questions

1 What special problems are likely to be faced by a manager on appointment to a new job as general administrative officer?

2 What factors do you consider enhance staff morale? Refer in your answer to staff seconded from their departments to assist with a major conference lasting over a three-day period.

3 In moving to new purpose-built premises considerable changes are to be made in the reception area which will now be staffed full-time. Discuss the administrative aspects likely to need consideration in drawing up a manual of procedures for the reception area.

4 A review is being made of individual workstations for clerical staff. List the likely features of such workstations and the points to bear in mind when designing such a position. You may, if you find it helpful, refer to a particular type of workstation with which you are familiar.

5 A manufacturer of consumer-durable goods (washing machines and vacuum cleaners) is considering setting up a depot in an area of the country previously supplied direct from the factory. What considerations will enter into the location and equipment of such a depot?

6 What are the major functions of the office within the organisation?

7 Attending an interview for an appointment in the retail trade, you are asked 'What are the main sources of stock losses in the retail trade field and what measures can be taken to reduce them?' Give a detailed reply, referring in particular to the security aspects of retail trade.

8 What is the use of each of the following copy invoices?
   a the top copy
   b the delivery note

c the advice note

d the 'gate' copy

e the second copy

f the representative's copy

See below for a suggested answer to this question.

9 Your managing director has asked you to recommend a site for a new office. What criteria would you consider in making your suggestions?

10 'An effective manager delegates his/her authority to his/her subordinates.' What is delegation and how should it be undertaken?

11 a What is aligned documentation in clerical activities?

b Explain how aligned documentation is achieved, the principles behind it and the advantages it brings to administrators.

12 As administrative officer you are chairman of a committee dealing with safety at work. The quarterly meeting is due to take place shortly. Outline the procedures for organising such a meeting.

# 11.6 Study tips: suggested answer to question 8

The uses of the various copies are:

1 *The top copy* It goes to the customer as evidence of the contract of sale between the two parties named on it, giving an accurate description of the goods, quantity, quality, price, and so on. It becomes the customer's purchases invoice for accounting purposes.

2 *The delivery note* It goes to stores and then to dispatch department where it is used to get a clear signature on delivery at destination.

3 *The advice note* It goes to the stores department so the goods can be picked out from stock and assembled for packing. The advice note is packed with the goods or, if this is impossible, it is attached to the goods by a tie-on envelope or other device. It enables the customer's stores to know what is supposed to be in the package, and to make out a goods received note for their purchasing department on arrival.

4 *The gate copy* It is used when goods are collected by customers (for example, at DIY builders' outlets) so that the gate-keeper can check the goods on board and ensure that only those items paid for are removed from the site.

5 *The second copy* It is the seller's accounts copy and goes to the accounts department to record the sales made and debit the debtor's account if the goods were sold on credit.

6 *The representative's copy* It goes to the representative who took the order to confirm its fulfilment, date of dispatch, and so on. This can be used on his/her next visit to the customer to confirm fulfilment, and often earns repeat orders because a busy customer says 'OK, repeat that order for me.'

# 12 Other responsibilities of the administrative officer

## 12.1 Revision test: other aspects of administration

(To consolidate your knowledge of Chapter 12 in the main text)

| Answers | Questions |
| --- | --- |
| | 1 What is an O&M department? |
| 1 An organisation and methods department, which reviews all systems in use from time to time and is available to investigate any new procedural problem and to advise upon difficulties revealed in production or distribution, criminal activity by staff, and so on. | 2 What are the stages in an O&M investigation? |
| 2 (a) The terms of reference are laid down for the investigation.<br>(b) The existing situation is investigated.<br>(c) This situation is then analysed for possible improvement.<br>(d) A new system is devised and fully documented by drawing up a proposed manual of procedures.<br>(e) Comments are invited.<br>(f) The final plan is presented to senior management and if approved is phased in gradually. | 3 What are the chief problems for most firms as far as security goes? |
| 3 (a) Opportunist theft<br>(b) burglary<br>(c) industrial espionage<br>(d) letter and parcel bombs<br>(e) computer theft<br>(f) care of keys<br>(g) Mis-use of the telephone and computer networks. | 4 What is industrial espionage? |
| 4 It is spying on a firm or company to discover secrets of every sort. They may be secret processes, new developments under research, sources of supply, important customers, bids and tenders for jobs, key personnel who could be head-hunted away, and so on. | 5 Whom should we suspect of industrial espionage? |
| 5 Without being paranoid about it, everyone. We need to be careful about visitors; make them sign in and out giving full details of their visit. Escort them from reception to the | *(continues opposite)* |

| Answers | Questions |
|---|---|
| person they are to see, and back again. Watch out for surveillance of premises, and for people offered a job who do not take it up, and so on. | **6 What do we call the climate in which a business operates?** |
| 6 Its environment. | **7 What are the chief aspects of a business's environment?** |
| 7 The economic, legal, social and political aspects, each of which exerts powerful influences on a business's activities and may make claims upon it. | **8 What is 'the concept of the claimant'?** |
| 8 It is a concept which holds that everyone inside an organisation and a great many outsiders in the general environment in which the organisation thrives may make claims from time to time upon it. A business administrator who understands the concept will be able to make sensible decisions about meeting, or rebutting, claims. | **9 Go over the test again until you are sure of all the answers. Then try the self-assessment questions below.** |

## 12.2  Self-assessment questions

(Answers at 12.4 below)

Here are nine questions about Chapter 12 in the main text. Take a sheet of paper and answer the questions. Then go through the self-assessment procedure for each question and give yourself a mark out of 100. File these sheets for revision later.

1  Why do large companies need an organisation and methods department?
2  What is opportunist theft?
3  What is industrial espionage? How can it be prevented?
4  Name four clues that might alert you to the fact that a packet is a letter bomb?
5  Why should an administrative officer be concerned about insurance?
6  What sort of risks are 'uninsurable'?
7  What are the chief aspects of any organisation's working environment?
8  Explain 'the concept of the claimant'.
9  What claims might an actress working for a touring theatrical company make upon the company?

## 12.3  An assignment on claimants

After studying Table 12.1 carefully, draw up an organisational claimant model for the firm for whom you work, or for the college or school where you are studying. What claims are likely to be made, in the widest possible meaning of the word 'claims', by those directly engaged in the organisation and by outsiders? Present your assignment as a written report to the managing director (or other senior official) with the table of claimants as the main body of the text.

# 12.4 Answers to self-assessment questions

1  Large companies develop many systems and sub-systems for carrying out their work and unless they are careful will waste both time and money in perpetuating activities which are no longer required, or could be done in a better way.

The organisation and methods department's functions are

a  to review periodically all systems used in an office, factory, and so on

b  to help design any new procedure or revision of an old procedure

c  to seek simple solutions to documentation and similar problems and thus promote efficiency and profitability.

In particular, the O&M department will consider the use of computerised methods wherever possible.

2  Opportunist theft is theft carried out on the spur of the moment, because the opportunity to steal presented itself, and the thief thought it would be a pity to pass it up. Examples are the theft of a car from a motorist who leaves his/her car running while fetching something from the house, or the delivery driver who leaves the door of the van open while he/she delivers part of a consignment.

3  Industrial espionage is spying, not for state secrets but for industrial secrets about designs, methods of work, chemical formulae, take-over activities, and so on. Many people have photographic memories, and a few seconds is all they need to reproduce plans, contracts, layouts of materials and machinery, and so on. The best way to defeat such activities is with a security-conscious staff and carefully thought-out procedures for the reception of visitors, escorting visitors to the person they are to speak to, entry barriers to various parts of the plant, and so on.

4  Four clues might be:

a  dishevelled appearance of the package

b  incorrect names or mis-spelled names

c  oil or grease marks

d  signs of wires or electrical connections

5  Insurance is a method of reducing the impact of losses by spreading risks over a large body of businesses. In return for a small premium from each firm covered, the unlucky members of the insured group will be compensated for the losses they suffer. An administrative officer will be keen to ensure that where a risk can be covered economically the necessary cover will be arranged. He/she will also wish to ensure that where insurance is compulsory (as with motor vehicle use, and employer's liability insurance) these obligations are met.

6  Uninsurable risks are those that cannot be reduced to a clear statistical probability. Thus we can calculate the likelihood of accidents to motorists, or bad weather on a particular day in June or December. We cannot calculate the probability that the proprietor will prove to be a fool in business matters, or that the public will dislike the designs we have made for our fashion show. These are examples of uninsurable risks.

7 The chief aspects of an organisation's working environment are the economic framework, the legal framework, the social framework and the political framework of the society in which it seeks to prosper.
8 The concept of the claimant is one that holds that at any time people both inside and outside a firm or organisation are likely to make claims of one sort or another upon it. An organisation should anticipate such claims and lay down policies for dealing with them, so that it is ready either to concede the claim and meet it or, alternatively, rebut the claim and fight it.
9 An actress might make, among others, the following claims:
   a to be paid her salary
   b to be paid subsistence money for board and lodging while on tour
   c to be paid travelling expenses (or to be reimbursed for petrol used)
   d to be insured against accidents while at work
   e to be provided with proper costumes for the parts to be played
   f to have pension contributions paid to an agreed scheme
   g to be accorded reasonable opportunities to meet the press, and proper billing on all posters, programmes, and so on.

# 12.5 Examination questions

1 What are the functions of the organisation and methods department? To what extent would the department consider computerisation when looking at the work of any part of the organisation under review?
2 List the chief aspects of office security procedures. What rules would you lay down to ensure safe handling of:
   a filing cabinet keys
   b computer terminals as part of a local area network (LAN).
3 Asked what was the most important qualification needed by those working on the installation of safes, the youth employment officer replied 'honesty'. Tomorrow you are to induct a group of new apprentices to work at the Very Secure Safe Co. Write a short section of your induction talk about 'honesty'.
4 What is industrial espionage? How can we prevent people stealing our secrets?
5 Insurance cannot reduce losses, all it can do is share them out more fairly so that the loss falls lightly upon many people, rather than heavily on a few. Explain.
6 The administration officer includes in his/her duties a general responsibility for reducing risks. What sort of risks might he/she watch out for day by day, and consider in particular at regular intervals as the year passes?
7 What is 'the business environment'? What considerations might need to be borne in mind by the chief administrative officer of an oil company on a riverside site with a large housing estate close by?
8 Explain 'the concept of the claimant'. Name ten different people, organisations or institutions which might be claimants on a large multinational corporation.

## 12.6  Study tips: suggested answer to question 3

We now come to a section of this talk about the company which is of crucial importance, and especially crucial to young people like yourselves. It concerns the whole question of honesty. We make safes, as our name 'The Very Secure Safe Co.' tells you, and the honesty of the people who work for us is of great importance. It isn't just a question of safe-keeping of money, although the vast majority of safes are used partly for that purpose. Other vital things are also stored in safes. For example, hospitals keep dangerous drugs in safes to prevent them falling into the wrong hands. Accountants keep the financial records of companies in their safes, and details of secret negotiations which must not be revealed to anyone for fear they start a panic on the stock exchange. It is a serious offense, called insider dealing, to reveal such information to anyone.

We must therefore warn you that very severe consequences will follow any instance of dishonesty on your part. We offer secure employment, and training in the manufacture and marketing of security devices of all sorts, at good rates of pay. In return you must give us honest work and keep our security arrangements and security devices absolutely secret. Do not talk about your work to anyone. Be on your guard against anyone trying to pump you for information and be scrupulously honest in your own affairs. Any sort of charge against you for any dishonest practice, even if nothing to do with this firm, would lead to a reconsideration of you as an employee, because it would raise the question as to whether you had become a security risk.

At the end of this session you will be asked to sign an induction form which lists the various matters brought up in this induction period, and including a mention of the need for honesty in this employment. When you sign this form you are undertaking a clear commitment to deal honestly with us and our customers. May I just add that if at any time you get into any financial difficulty, you should come and see us at once and discuss the matter. We are sure to be able to sort out most ordinary problems, and we really do need to be told in good time before any financial difficulty becomes burdensome. All such problems will of course be dealt with in the strictest confidence.